SEASONS IN THE HOME

SUMMER

CREATIVE
HOME
ARTS
—CLUB—

CREATIVE HOME ARTS LIBRARY™

SUM

CREATIVE
HOME
ARTS
—CLUB—

CREATIVE HOME ARTS CLUB
MINNETONKA, MINNESOTA

CREDITS

SEASONS IN THE HOME
SUMMER

Printed in 2004.

Tom Carpenter
Creative Director

Julie Cisler
Book Design & Production

Michele Stockham
Senior Book Development Coordinator

Heather Koshiol
Managing Editor

2 3 4 5 6 / 07 06 05 04
ISBN 1-58159-203-5
© 2003 Creative Home Arts Club

Creative Home Arts Club
12301 Whitewater Drive
Minnetonka, Minnesota 55343
www.creativehomeartsclub.com

Contributing Writers
Bonnie Blodgett
Alan Branhagen
Carole Brown
Lars Dalsgaard
Mary Evans
Jana Freiband
Zoe Graul
Patsy Jamieson
Michele Anna Jordan
Lisa Lensegrav
Colleen Miner
Cheryl Natt
Yula Nelson
Kelly O'Hara
Beatrice Ojakangas
Ellen Spector Platt
Barbara Pleasant
Kathleen Prisant
Mark Scarbrough
John Schumacher
Bruce Weinstein

Contributing Photographers
Bill Lindner Photography
Phil Aarrestad Photography
Tad Ware & Company, INC.

Illustrator
Nancy Wirsig McClure/Hand-To-Mouse Arts

Additional Photography
Jim Block
David Cavagnaro
Walter Chandoha
Chuck Crandall and Barbara Crandall
Rosalind Creasy
Alan and Linda Detrick
Derek Fell
Harry Haralambou
Margaret Hensel
Saxon Holt
John Mowers Photography
Maggie Oster
Barbara Pleasant
Positive Images: Jerry Howard

CONTENTS

SEASONS IN THE HOME

SUMMER

INTRODUCTION

Everyone loves summer. Sun, warmth, carefree laughter, lazy-hot days, a cool drink on the porch, a nap under a shade tree ... no matter what summer means to you, it is the best of seasons.

It's true that summer was made for relaxing. And to enjoy a vacation or some long weekends, too. But summer is also one of the best times to be at home. As much as the beautiful weather gets a person ready to slow down or escape, it energizes a soul too. There are so many wonderful things to do!

Summer cooking takes on a casual, fresh and delicious flair. Creating summery crafts from flowers, vegetables and other natural materials becomes an addictive pastime. The season's flowers and outdoorsy focus offer opportunities to decorate in fun and innovative ways. Gardening is a warm-weather rite. And when some of the festivities can be held in the glory of the outdoors, there's no better time to entertain guests.

Those are the ideas behind *Seasons in the Home — Summer*, and the idea-filled, picture-packed pages ahead. This book will help you cook some of the year's best food, create great craft projects that utilize summer's bounty, make your home (both inside and out) a beautiful and inviting place, experience your biggest gardening successes to date, and do warm-weather entertaining like a pro.

It's all about ideas. It's all about you. It's all about summer. Enjoy this one-of-a-kind season in *your* home.

SUMMER COOKING

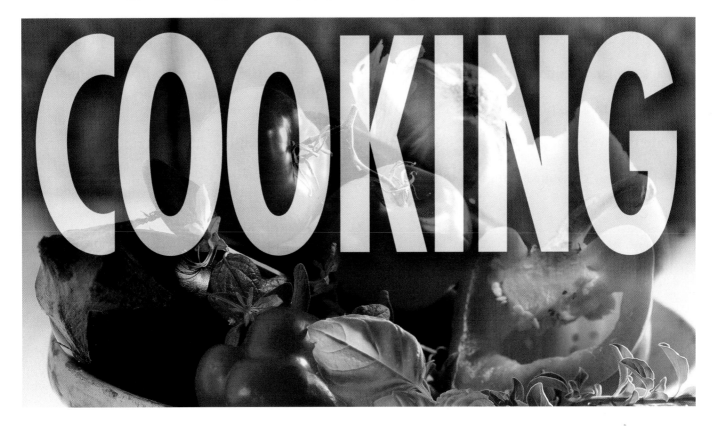

Y ou really can *taste* summer. Using fresh and whole-some ingredients, and cooking in simple and easy ways, produces food creations that burst with the flavors of the season. Summer cooking our way leaves you time to enjoy everything else the season has to offer, too. From breakfasts and appetizers to main dishes on the grill, beverages and cool desserts, you're going to love cooking with these recipes.

Facing page: Fresh Tomato Salad with Pesto Croutons, page 20

BAKED EGGS WITH TARRAGON

Celebrate the return of tarragon in your garden by making this simple French egg dish for a summer breakfast. To make the cream topping, thin low-fat sour cream with milk because the mixture has a light tang that is reminiscent of crème fraîche (you'll appreciate the lower fat content), but if you have whipping cream on hand, substitute 4 tablespoons for the sour cream and milk.

4   eggs
    Dash of salt
    Dash of freshly ground pepper
4   teaspoons chopped fresh tarragon
2   tablespoons reduced-fat sour cream
2   tablespoons reduced-fat milk

1 Heat oven to 325°F. Heat tea kettle of water to a boil. Spray 4 (6-oz. or ⅓-cup) custard cups or ramekins with cooking spray.

2 Carefully crack 1 egg into each custard cup; season lightly with salt and pepper. Sprinkle each egg with 1 teaspoon tarragon.

3 Place sour cream in small bowl; gradually add milk, whisking until smooth. Top each egg with 1 tablespoon sour cream mixture.

4 Place custard cups in small baking dish with sides. Add enough boiling water to come one-fourth of the way up sides of custard cups. Place baking dish in oven; cover loosely with sheet of parchment paper or aluminum foil.

5 Bake 10 to 14 minutes or just until eggs are set. Serve immediately.

Serves 4.
Preparation time: 15 minutes.
Ready to serve: 30 minutes.
Per serving: 90 calories, 5.5 g total fat (2 g saturated fat), 215 mg cholesterol, 145 mg sodium, 0 g fiber.

Chef's Notes

- Use any delicate fresh-flavored herb, such as chervil, chives, basil or dill, alone or in a combination, such as *fines herbes* (a mixture of finely chopped herbs such as chervil, chives, parsley and tarragon).

- Timing baked eggs can be tricky — they turn from nicely set to hard in a flash — so monitor them carefully. To test, touch eggs lightly with your finger; whites should be firm around the edges and yolks should not be runny, but not too firm either.

POTATO, RED BELL PEPPER AND ONION FRITTATA

This open-faced omelet is a practical way to serve several people at once. To save time, cook the onion, pepper and potatoes in advance. When you're ready to make the omelet, heat the vegetables in the skillet, pour in the eggs and continue with the recipe.

12	large eggs
¼	cup water
¾	lb. potatoes
2	tablespoons olive oil
1	medium onion, sliced
1	red bell pepper, sliced
2	tablespoons minced fresh rosemary
1	teaspoon dried thyme
1	teaspoon salt
¼	teaspoon freshly ground pepper
2	garlic cloves, minced
1	tablespoon chopped fresh parsley

1 In large bowl, whisk eggs with water until blended.

2 Scrub and peel potatoes. Cut into ⅛-inch slices or small cubes; cover with water in large pot. Cook potatoes over medium-high heat until fork-tender.

3 Heat oil in large skillet over medium heat. Sauté onions and bell pepper 5 minutes, stirring occasionally until onions start to brown.

4 Drain potatoes; pat dry. Add potatoes, rosemary, thyme, ½ of the teaspoon salt, the pepper and onions to bell peppers; toss 5 minutes, stirring frequently. Cover skillet loosely; cook an additional 5 minutes. Stir 3 or 4 times. Sample potatoes. If they are soft, add garlic; if not, continue to cook until softened. Toss vegetables with garlic and cook 2 to 3 minutes until garlic is fragrant.

5 Heat broiler. Stir remaining ½ teaspoon salt and 1 tablespoon chopped parsley into beaten eggs. Pour into skillet, spreading vegetables evenly. Reduce heat to low; cook eggs slowly. Run spatula around edge to loosen omelet from pan, allowing uncooked egg to spill over edge to bottom of skillet. Cook 10 minutes or until bottom and sides of omelet have set.

6 Place skillet under broiler, turning as necessary for even cooking. Broil about 4 minutes or until top of omelet is lightly browned and eggs are slightly puffy. Cut omelet into wedges. Garnish with additional parsley.

Serves 6 to 8.
Preparation time: 30 minutes.
Ready to serve: 1 hour.
Per serving: 310 calories, 23.5 g total fat (6.5 g saturated fat), 440 mg cholesterol, 580 mg sodium, 2 g fiber.

HERBED GOAT CHEESE SPREAD

Goat cheese seasoned with dried herbs is widely available in cheese stores and supermarkets these days. Herbed goat cheese, however, is so much better when you make your own with the fresh herbs of summer. Accompany this recipe with toasted French bread.

6	oz. creamy goat cheese
1	tablespoon extra-virgin olive oil
¼	cup chopped fresh chives
3	tablespoons chopped fresh parsley
1	tablespoon chopped fresh savory, if desired
1	small garlic clove, minced

1 In medium bowl, beat goat cheese at medium speed until smooth and creamy. Add oil; beat until smooth. Add chives, parsley, savory and garlic; mix with rubber spatula. (Spread can be prepared up to 2 days ahead. Cover and refrigerate.)

Serves 6 (1 tablespoon servings).
Preparation time: 20 minutes.
Ready to serve: 20 minutes.
Per serving: 60 calories, 5 g total fat (2.5 g saturated fat), 15 mg cholesterol, 60 mg sodium, 0 g fiber.

Chef's Note

- To make attractive bite-sized goat cheese "truffles," use a melon baller to scoop out small balls of herbed goat cheese about 1 inch in diameter. With lightly oiled hands, form balls into smooth truffles. Roll and coat half the balls in chopped parsley, the other half in chopped pitted black olives.

CHERRY TOMATOES FILLED WITH PESTO CREAM CHEESE

This is a perfect appetizer to serve in summer when addictive cherry tomatoes and fresh basil are at their peak.

2	medium garlic cloves, crushed
1	teaspoon kosher (coarse) salt
3	cups fresh basil leaves
⅓	cup pine nuts plus 2 tablespoons, toasted*
¼	teaspoon freshly ground pepper
1	tablespoon extra-virgin olive oil
1	(8-oz.) pkg. reduced-fat cream cheese, cut into chunks
2	pints cherry tomatoes
48	fresh basil leaves (2 cups)

1. Using mortar and pestle or side of chef's knife, mash garlic and salt into a paste. In food processor, combine 3 cups basil, ⅓ cup pine nuts, pepper and mashed garlic mixture; process until pine nuts are ground. With motor running, drizzle in olive oil. Add cream cheese; pulse until smooth and creamy. (Filling can be prepared up to 2 days ahead. Cover and refrigerate.)

2. Shortly before serving,** with serrated or sharp paring knife, cut an X on rounded side (opposite stem) of each tomato. Using grapefruit spoon or your fingertips, scoop out seeds, taking care to keep tomatoes intact.

3. Place filling in pastry bag fitted with star tip or small plastic food bag with ½-inch hole cut in corner. Pipe rosette of filling into each tomato cavity. Set each filled tomato on basil leaf; arrange on serving platter. Garnish each with pine nut.

About 48 appetizers.
Preparation time: 35 minutes.
Ready to serve: 35 minutes.
Per serving: 25 calories, 2 g total fat (0.5 g saturated fat), 0 mg cholesterol, 60 mg sodium, 0.5 g fiber.

Cooking Tips

* To toast pine nuts, heat small, heavy skillet over medium-low heat. Add pine nuts and stir constantly 2 to 3 minutes or until light golden and fragrant. Transfer to a small bowl and let cool.

** Wait until shortly before serving to stuff the tomatoes. Cherry tomatoes lose their charm once they have been refrigerated.

Chef's Note

• Try cherry tomatoes stuffed with *Herbed Goat Cheese Spread* (page 12).

ASPARAGUS SALAD WITH MINT AND ALMONDS

During asparagus season, serve this prized vegetable as a special course. A light lemon vinaigrette highlighted with mint and toasted almonds showcases asparagus beautifully.

Lemon Dressing
1	small garlic clove, crushed
¼	teaspoon salt
2	tablespoons fresh lemon juice
3	tablespoons extra-virgin olive oil
½	teaspoon honey
⅛	teaspoon freshly ground pepper

Salad
1½	lb. asparagus, stem ends snapped
3	tablespoons chopped scallions
3	tablespoons slivered fresh mint
3	tablespoons slivered almonds (1 oz.), toasted*

1 Using mortar and pestle or side of chef's knife, mash garlic and salt into a paste. Transfer to small bowl. Whisk in lemon juice, oil, honey and pepper.

2 Place asparagus in steamer basket over boiling water. Steam, covered, 3 to 6 minutes or until tender-crisp. Rinse thoroughly under cold running water. Drain and pat dry.

3 To serve, arrange asparagus on serving platter. Spoon dressing over top. Sprinkle with scallions, mint and almonds.

Serves 4.
Preparation time: 20 minutes.
Ready to serve: 25 minutes.
Per serving: 155 calories, 13.5 g total fat (1.5 g saturated fat), 0 mg cholesterol, 150 mg sodium, 2.5 g fiber.

Cooking Tip

* To toast slivered almonds, spread in small baking pan. Bake at 375°F 5 to 10 minutes or until golden and fragrant. Transfer to small bowl and let cool.

HERB GARDEN SALAD

Of course, fresh herbs make a great addition to any dressing, but supplementing greens with a lively and generous mixture of torn herb leaves is one of the best ways to give delightful herbal fragrance to a summer salad. To showcase the flavor of the herbs, use a delicate lettuce like Boston, rather than stronger-tasting mesclun greens.

Vinaigrette
- 4 teaspoons tarragon vinegar or white wine vinegar
- 2 tablespoons finely chopped shallots
- ½ teaspoon Dijon mustard
- ¼ teaspoon salt
- ⅛ teaspoon freshly ground pepper
  Dash of sugar
- ¼ cup extra-virgin olive oil

Salad
- 1 garlic clove, halved
- 2 medium heads butterhead (Boston or Bibb) lettuce leaves, torn into bite-sized pieces (8 cups)
- 1 cup fresh Italian parsley leaves, torn into ½-inch pieces
- 1 cup assorted herb leaves, torn into ½-inch pieces (burnet, chervil, lovage, tarragon, etc.)
- ½ cup chopped chives
- 12 unsprayed edible flowers (chive blossoms, nasturtiums, etc.), if desired

1 In small jar with tight-fitting lid, combine vinegar, shallots, mustard, salt, pepper and sugar. Cover jar; shake to blend. Add oil; shake to blend. (Dressing can be prepared up to 2 days ahead. Cover and refrigerate.)

2 Rub large salad bowl with cut sides of garlic clove. Place lettuce, parsley, assorted herbs and chives in bowl. Just before serving, drizzle dressing over salad; toss well. Garnish with flowers.

Serves 6 (2-cup servings).
Preparation time: 25 minutes.
Ready to serve: 25 minutes.
Per serving: 95 calories, 9.5 g total fat (1.5 g saturated fat), 0 mg cholesterol, 115 mg sodium, 1.5 g fiber.

Chef's Note
- To keep washed greens and herbs fresh for up to 1 hour, place a damp kitchen towel over the salad bowl. For longer storage, refrigerate salad for up to 8 hours. If there is not enough room in the refrigerator for a large salad bowl, keep salad cool for several hours by placing a nonwooden salad bowl in a larger pan of ice water.

SUMMER GARDEN SALAD

Making this salad may become a summer ritual when the best of the produce is at its peak.

The vegetables don't really need to be cooked, just "licked" with the flames until golden

brown, creating a toasty-sweet flavor.

1 cob corn, husks and silk removed
1 small red onion, quartered
2 firm tomatoes (use heirloom tomatoes, if
   available)
1 tablespoon plus 1 teaspoon kosher (coarse)
   salt
1 (8-oz.) pkg. corkscrew pasta (fusilli)
¾ cup fresh basil, torn
3 garlic cloves
¼ teaspoon freshly ground pepper
¼ teaspoon white wine vinegar
¼ cup extra-virgin olive oil
1 lb. crostini

1 Heat grill. Cook corn and onion 4 to 6 inches from heat, turning occasionally, 10 minutes. Add tomatoes to grill. Cook 5 minutes or just until slightly softened but not cooked through, turning occasionally. Remove from grill; let cool.

2 Meanwhile, fill large pot ⅔ full of water; add 1 tablespoon of the salt. Bring to a boil over high heat. Add pasta; cook 15 minutes or until al dente. Drain. Rinse thoroughly in cool water; drain. Transfer to large bowl.

3 Cut kernels from corn; cut onion into 1-inch pieces. Peel tomatoes; seed and coarsely chop. In large bowl, combine pasta, corn, onion, tomatoes and basil; toss well.

4 Using mortar and pestle or side of chef's knife, mash garlic, remaining 1 teaspoon salt and pepper into a paste; transfer to small bowl. Stir in vinegar; mix well. Gradually whisk in olive oil. Add to pasta mixture; toss. Serve with crostini.

Serves 6 (1-cup servings).
Preparation time: 15 minutes.
Ready to serve: 45 minutes.
Per serving: 505 calories, 17.5 g total fat (2.5 g saturated fat), 0 mg cholesterol, 900 mg sodium, 5 g fiber.

CRAB LOUIS SANDWICH

Like Dungeness crab, from which it is prepared, *Crab Louis* is a West Coast classic. Piled

into sourdough rolls, Crab Louis becomes part summer salad and part summer sandwich.

¾ cup mayonnaise
3 tablespoons bottled chili sauce
½ teaspoon Worcestershire sauce
3 tablespoons finely chopped green onions
2 tablespoons finely chopped green bell pepper
1 tablespoon fresh lemon juice
⅛ teaspoon salt
⅛ teaspoon freshly ground pepper
1 lb. fresh Dungeness crabmeat
4 sourdough rolls
2 cups shredded iceberg lettuce
2 small tomatoes, cut into wedges
2 tablespoons chopped fresh chives

1 In small bowl, combine mayonnaise, chili sauce, Worcestershire sauce, green onions, bell pepper, lemon juice, salt and pepper.

2 Place crabmeat in large bowl. Add ½ cup of the dressing; gently toss without breaking up crabmeat.

3 Cut each sourdough roll in half horizontally. Partially hollow each roll by removing some of the crumbs, leaving 1-inch-thick shell.

4 Arrange ½ cup shredded lettuce on each of 4 salad plates. Top each with hollowed roll. Spoon about ½ cup crabmeat mixture into each roll. Tilt top of roll to the side.

5 Arrange tomato wedges around roll; sprinkle with chives. Serve remaining dressing on the side.

4 sandwiches.
Preparation time: 20 minutes.
Ready to serve: 30 minutes.
Per serving: 520 calories, 32 g total fat (4.5 g saturated fat), 155 mg cholesterol, 1045 mg sodium, 3 g fiber.

FRESH TOMATO SALAD WITH PESTO CROUTONS

Try these tasty croutons in your favorite tomato soup or with other summer salads. But they're absolutely perfect with this wonderful *Fresh Tomato Salad*.

Croutons

¼   cup extra-virgin olive oil
¼   cup lightly packed, coarsely chopped fresh basil leaves
2   tablespoons freshly grated Parmesan cheese
6   (¾-inch) slices stale baguette, cut into ¾-inch cubes

Dressing

2   tablespoons extra-virgin olive oil
1   tablespoon lemon juice
¼   teaspoon salt
⅛   teaspoon freshly ground pepper

Salad

¼   cup chopped red onion
4   cups torn leaf lettuce
3   medium red tomatoes, sliced
3   medium yellow tomatoes, sliced

1 Place ¼ cup oil, basil and cheese in blender or food processor. Pulse to puree. Pour into medium bowl. Add bread; toss to coat. Heat large skillet over medium-high heat until hot. Add bread; cook 5 to 7 minutes or until brown and crispy, turning often. Set aside.

2 In small bowl whisk together oil, lemon juice, salt and pepper. Set aside.

3 Place onion in another small bowl; cover with cold water. Soak 15 minutes; drain well. Spread lettuce over serving platter. Top with overlapping rows of tomatoes, alternating colors and beginning with a row of red tomatoes. Repeat until all tomatoes are used. Sprinkle with onion; drizzle with dressing. Sprinkle with croutons.

Serves 6.
Preparation time: 15 minutes. Ready to serve: 30 minutes.
Per serving: 200 calories, 15 g total fat (2.5 g saturated fat), 0 mg cholesterol, 235 mg sodium, 2.5 g fiber.

BLACK BEAN SALAD WITH CILANTRO PESTO

Canned, roasted green peppers work well in cilantro pesto, making this a quick salad to assemble. Add roasted chicken strips for a healthy one-dish meal that's simple and quick to prepare on any busy (or not-so-busy) summer day.

1 cup fresh chopped cilantro
¼ cup canned roasted green peppers, drained, rinsed (or ½ fresh green bell pepper, roasted and peeled)
1 tablespoon fresh lime juice
1 garlic clove, mashed
½ teaspoon salt
¼ cup extra-virgin olive oil
3 (15-oz.) cans black beans, rinsed and drained
1 cup cherry tomatoes, quartered
½ cup peeled, diced jicama
½ yellow bell pepper, cut into 1-inch strips
2 teaspoons fresh lime juice
2 teaspoons extra-virgin olive oil
½ teaspoon chili powder
Tortilla chips, garnish

1 In blender, combine cilantro, roasted pepper, 1 tablespoon lime juice, garlic and salt. Cover and blend until chunky. With blender running, add ¼ cup oil in a steady stream.

2 In medium bowl, combine black beans and cilantro dressing. Toss to coat.

3 In medium bowl, combine cherry tomatoes, jicama and yellow bell pepper. Add 2 teaspoons lime juice and 2 teaspoons olive oil; toss to coat. Spoon tomato mixture over beans. Sprinkle with chili powder.

4 Just before serving, surround salad with tortilla chips.

Serves 6 (1-cup servings).
Preparation time: 15 minutes.
Ready to serve: 20 minutes.
Per serving: 340 calories, 12.5 g total fat (2 g saturated fat), 0 mg cholesterol, 585 mg sodium, 12 g fiber.

GREEN RICE

A rice pilaf seasoned with onion, garlic, cilantro and mild chiles makes a perfect summer accompaniment to most any Latin dish.

2   teaspoons olive oil
1   medium onion, chopped
1   (4.5-oz.) can chopped green chiles
2   garlic cloves, minced
1   cup long-grain white rice
1   (14.5-oz.) can reduced-sodium chicken broth
¾   cup chopped fresh cilantro
½   cup chopped trimmed scallions
1   tablespoon fresh lime juice
⅛   teaspoon salt
⅛   teaspoon freshly ground pepper

1 In medium saucepan, heat oil over medium heat until hot. Add onion; cook about 2 to 3 minutes or until tender, stirring frequently. Add chiles and garlic; cook 1 minute, stirring frequently. Add rice; cook 1 minute, stirring constantly, until well mixed. Add broth; bring to a simmer over medium heat. Reduce heat to low; simmer, covered, about 20 minutes or until rice is tender and liquid has been absorbed. Remove from heat. Add cilantro, scallions, lime juice, salt and pepper; fluff and mix gently with rubber spatula.

Serves 4 (1-cup servings).
Preparation time: 10 minutes.
Ready to serve: 40 minutes.
Per serving: 245 calories, 3.5 g total fat (0.5 g saturated fat), 0 mg cholesterol, 570 mg sodium, 2 g fiber.

RATATOUILLE PEPPERS

Visit your local farmers' market in late summer to find the ingredients you need for this dish. Turn these peppers into a delicious vegetarian entrée by serving two stuffed pepper halves per person, along with a fresh, tossed salad and French bread. You can also serve these peppers as side dishes with grilled tuna steaks or other meats.

3	tablespoons olive oil
1	large onion (about ½ lb.), chopped
1	tablespoon minced garlic
½	lb. peeled eggplant, cut into 1-inch pieces (3 cups)
½	lb. zucchini, cut into 1-inch pieces (2 cups)
1	yellow or orange bell pepper (about ½ lb.), cut into 1-inch pieces
2	large tomatoes (about 1 lb.), peeled, cut into 1-inch pieces
¼	cup chopped fresh basil
½	teaspoon salt
¼	teaspoon freshly ground pepper
3	red bell peppers, halved, seeded
3	tablespoons freshly grated Parmesan cheese

1 Heat oil in nonreactive Dutch oven over medium-high heat until hot. Add onion; sauté 3 to 4 minutes or until softened. Add garlic; sauté an additional minute or until fragrant. Add eggplant, zucchini and yellow bell pepper; sauté an additional 4 to 5 minutes. Add tomatoes, basil, salt and pepper. Reduce heat to low; cook, covered, 15 minutes, stirring occasionally. Uncover; increase heat to medium. Cook about 10 to 15 minutes or until almost all cooking liquid has evaporated. Dish may be made up to 1 day ahead to this point. Cover and refrigerate.

2 Heat oven to 350°F. Line baking sheet with foil. Place red bell peppers cut-side up on baking sheet. Divide ratatouille mixture evenly among peppers. Top with cheese. Bake about 30 minutes or until peppers are crisp-tender and ratatouille is hot.

Serves 6.
Preparation time: 40 minutes.
Ready to serve: 1 hour, 25 minutes.
Per serving: 130 calories, 8 g total fat (1.5 g saturated fat), 0 mg cholesterol, 260 mg sodium, 3.5 g fiber.

SPRING ROLLS WITH SHRIMP AND RICE NOODLE FILLING

These lively and light Vietnamese spring rolls make ideal hot-weather fare. Cilantro and mint provide a fresh contrast to the spicy dipping sauce.

Dressing

½   cup pineapple juice
2   tablespoons low-sodium soy sauce
1   tablespoon fish sauce
2   tablespoons rice vinegar
1   tablespoon canola oil
1   teaspoon Thai green curry paste
1   teaspoon packed brown sugar
3   tablespoons coarsely chopped fresh ginger
2   medium garlic cloves, crushed

Spring Rolls

2   oz. thin rice noodles or rice sticks
12   rice-paper wrappers
12   large leaves Boston lettuce
1   lb. shelled, deveined cooked medium shrimp, tails removed
¾   cup grated carrots (2 to 3 medium)
¾   cup finely diced fresh pineapple
¾   cup slivered fresh cilantro
¾   cup slivered fresh mint

Chef's Notes

- Fish sauce, green curry paste, rice vermicelli and rice-paper wrappers can be found in the Asian section of many supermarkets, health food stores and Asian markets.
- For an interesting presentation, wrap each spring roll with a ribbon of chives.
- Whole shrimp look attractive. But for easier wrapping, chop them coarsely and use about 2 tablespoons per roll.

1 In blender, combine pineapple juice, soy sauce, fish sauce, rice vinegar, oil, curry paste, brown sugar, ginger and garlic; process until well blended. (Dressing can be made ahead. Cover and refrigerate up to 2 days.)

2 In large bowl, cover rice noodles with boiling water; stir to immerse and separate strands. Let soak 5 minutes. Drain noodles; rinse with cold water. Drain again, shaking colander to release excess water. Return noodles to bowl. Add 2 tablespoons of the dressing; toss to coat.

3 Shortly before serving, assemble spring rolls. Set all prepared filling ingredients out on counter. Set out large bowl of warm water, baking sheet, serving platter and damp kitchen towel. Working with 2 rice-paper wrappers at a time, dip into warm water 10 to 20 seconds or until softened. Shake off moisture and lay out on baking sheet. Place one lettuce leaf on bottom third of each wrapper. Top each lettuce leaf with about 2 tablespoons rice noodle mixture, 3 or 4 shrimp, generous 1 tablespoon carrot, generous 1 tablespoon pineapple, 1 tablespoon cilantro and 1 tablespoon mint. Fold bottom of wrapper over to partially cover filling. Fold sides over filling and continue to roll wrapper into a cylinder to seal.

4 Place on platter. Cover with damp kitchen towel to prevent spring rolls from drying out. Repeat with remaining rice-paper wrappers and filling ingredients. Serve with remaining dressing as dipping sauce.

Serves 6.
Preparation time: 1 hour, 30 minutes.
Ready to serve: 1 hour, 30 minutes.
Per serving: 210 calories, 3.5 g total fat (0.5 g saturated fat), 155 mg cholesterol, 490 mg sodium, 2 g fiber.

CHICKEN QUESADILLAS WITH AVOCADO-TOMATO SALSA

When cut into eighths, these quesadillas make a wonderful appetizer for any summer gathering. Top them with *Avocado-Tomato Salsa*, some of the freshest and liveliest salsa you'll ever taste!

Chicken Quesadillas
2   cups cooked shredded chicken
¼   cup chopped fresh cilantro
8   (10-inch) flour tortillas
2   tablespoons vegetable oil
1   cup (4 oz.) shredded Monterey Jack cheese
1   (4-oz.) can chopped green chiles, drained

Avocado-Tomato Salsa
1   teaspoon ground cumin
1   garlic clove, minced
1½   teaspoons fresh lime juice
½   teaspoon finely chopped jalapeño chile
¼   cup chopped green onions
¼   teaspoon salt
¼   teaspoon freshly ground pepper
1   tablespoon chopped fresh cilantro
1   cup finely chopped, drained, vine-ripened tomatoes
1   small ripe avocado, pitted, finely chopped

1 **Chicken Quesadillas:** In small bowl, combine chicken and cilantro; mix well.

2 Brush 4 tortillas with oil. Top each with ¼ chicken mixture, ¼ cup cheese and 2 tablespoons chiles. Spread mixture to within ½ inch of edge of tortilla. Top each with another tortilla; brush top with oil.

3 Brush large skillet with oil. Cook each quesadilla over medium-high heat 4 to 6 minutes, turning once after 2 minutes, until light golden brown.

4 Cut each quesadilla on cutting board into quarters. Serve with Avocado-Tomato Salsa.

5 **Avocado-Tomato Salsa:** In medium bowl, combine cumin, garlic, lime juice, jalapeño, onions, salt, pepper, cilantro, tomatoes and avocado; mix well. Cover and let stand at room temperature 1 hour.

Serves 4.
Preparation time: 15 minutes.
Ready to serve: 1 hour, 10 minutes.
Per serving: 655 calories, 32.5 g total fat (9.5 g saturated fat), 83 mg cholesterol, 1450 mg sodium, 6 g fiber.

INSIDE-OUT CHEESEBURGERS

Everyone likes cheeseburgers, but they're a mess on the grill. So put the cheese *inside* the patties! Let these burgers rest just a few minutes before serving, because the cheese super-heats, the way it does on a pizza.

¼   cup (1 oz.) shredded cheddar cheese, at room temperature
¼   cup (1 oz.) crumbled blue cheese, preferably Gorgonzola, at room temperature
1½ lb. lean ground beef
1   tablespoon plus 1 teaspoon Worcestershire sauce
1   teaspoon sweet paprika
    Vegetable oil for grill grate, plus additional for buns
4   hamburger buns, halved

1 Heat grill for direct cooking. In small bowl, mix cheddar cheese and blue cheese. In large bowl, mix ground beef, Worcestershire and paprika with wooden spoon until uniform. Divide into 8 equal portions. Place on parchment paper; flatten each into 4-inch-long round, ¼ inch thick. Spread one-fourth of cheese mixture (about 2 tablespoons) onto each of 4 patties, leaving ½-inch border around edges. Cover each with remaining patty, crimping edges so cheese won't leak when grilled. Pat to seal.

2 Brush grill grate with oil. Place patties on gas grill directly over high heat or on charcoal grill 4 to 6 inches directly over high-heat coals. Grill, turning once with metal spatula, 8 to 10 minutes or until cooked through. Transfer to carving board; let rest 5 minutes. Brush cut side of buns with oil; place on grill grate, cut-side down, over high heat. Toast about 1 minute or until browned. Serve burgers on buns with condiments of your choice.

Serves 4.
Preparation time: 20 minutes.
Ready to serve: 30 minutes.
Per serving: 415 calories, 30 g total fat (12.5 g saturated fat), 110 mg cholesterol, 285 mg sodium, 0 g fiber.

Variations

Mix one of the following into the cheese mixture before placing it in the patties:

- 2 tablespoons crumbled cooked bacon or bacon-flavored bits
- 1 tablespoon dehydrated minced onion
- 1 tablespoon fresh thyme
- 2 teaspoons finely chopped roasted peanuts
- 2 teaspoons finely chopped toasted hazelnuts or walnuts
- ½ teaspoon garlic powder
- 4 drops hot pepper sauce
- 1 green onion, finely minced
- Or finely shred or crumble any one of the following cheeses and substitute it for Gorgonzola: Asiago, Boursin, Brie, Buffalo mozzarella, Monterey Jack, Parmesan, Provolone, Roblechon, soft goat cheese or Swiss.

GRILLED FISH AND EGGPLANT ROMA

Become an Italian grill chef with this fun and easy recipe. Everything here is so fresh and

bursting with taste, it truly *is* like taking a bite of summer.

4   (2- to 3-oz.) boneless skinless fish steaks
4   slices red onion (½ inch thick)
4   slices eggplant (½ inch thick)
4   red bell peppers, sliced into ½-inch-thick
    rings
8   slices tomato (1 inch thick)
½   cup olive oil
1   (28-oz.) can spaghetti sauce
⅛   teaspoon salt
⅛   teaspoon freshly ground pepper
1   tablespoon chopped fresh cilantro
1   tablespoon chopped fresh basil
3   cups (12 oz.) freshly grated mozzarella cheese

1 Heat grill.

2 Brush steaks, onions, eggplant, bell peppers and tomatoes with oil. Place spaghetti sauce in small saucepan on side of grill. Place onions and eggplant on gas grill over medium heat or on charcoal grill 4 to 6 inches from medium coals. Cook 3 minutes on each side.

3 Add steaks, bell peppers and tomatoes to grill; cook 2 minutes on each side or until steaks flake easily with a fork. Turn and season with salt and pepper. Cook an additional 2 minutes.

4 Remove onions, eggplant, steaks, bell peppers and tomatoes from grill.

5 Arrange eggplant on clean large platter. Layer with steaks and bell peppers. Spoon ½ tablespoon of the spaghetti sauce over each bell pepper ring. Add 1 steak to each bell pepper ring. Top each with onion and more sauce to taste. Evenly season with salt, pepper, cilantro and basil. Add tomato slices and more sauce to taste. Sprinkle with cheese.

Serves 4.
Preparation time: 20 minutes.
Ready to serve: 45 minutes.
Per serving: 675 calories, 38 g total fat (12 g saturated fat), 105 mg cholesterol, 1970 mg sodium, 7 g fiber.

Chef's Note

- Use your imagination with all your favorite vegetables and spices instead of what is listed here. Summer cooking is for fun. You don't have to follow the rules all the time!

SALMON WITH LEMON ROSAMARINA

You can prepare fresh tuna, swordfish and shark the same way you make the salmon here. Experiment and have fun with any of summer's fresh fish, maybe even something you catch yourself! Always start with fillets.

Lemon Butter
½ cup unsalted butter, softened
3 tablespoons minced lemon peel
1 tablespoon minced fresh Italian parsley
2 garlic cloves, crushed
½ teaspoon kosher (coarse) salt
½ teaspoon freshly ground pepper

Rosamarina
1 tablespoon kosher (coarse) salt plus more to taste
1 (8-oz.) pkg. rosamarina
3 tablespoons Lemon Butter, cut into pieces
Freshly ground pepper to taste

Salmon
2 tablespoons butter
1 (1½-lb.) boneless skinless salmon fillet, cut into 1-inch pieces
1 tablespoon minced lemon peel
¾ teaspoon minced fresh rosemary
Kosher (coarse) salt to taste
Freshly ground pepper to taste
4 small rosemary sprigs
1 lemon, cut in wedges

1 **Lemon Butter:** In food processor, pulse butter and seasonings until evenly mixed. Transfer to sheet of parchment paper. Shape into log about 1¼ inches in diameter. Roll parchment around butter; roll butter package in plastic wrap. Refrigerate up to 5 days or freeze up to 3 weeks.

2 **Rosamarina:** Fill large pot two-thirds full of water; add 1 tablespoon salt. Bring to a boil over high heat. Cook rosamarina according to package directions; drain. Transfer to warm serving bowl.

3 Add Lemon Butter to pasta; toss until melted. Season with salt and pepper. Set aside.

4 **Salmon:** In large skillet, melt butter over high heat. Cook salmon, tossing frequently, 3 to 4 minutes or until salmon flakes easily with fork. Add lemon peel and rosemary needles. Season with salt and pepper; toss 2 or 3 times. Remove from heat.

5 Divide rosamarina evenly among 4 plates; top each serving with salmon. Garnish with rosemary sprigs and lemon wedges.

Serves 4.
Preparation time: 10 minutes.
Ready to serve: 20 minutes.
Per serving: 530 calories, 22 g total fat (9 g saturated fat), 110 mg cholesterol, 470 mg sodium, 2.5 g fiber.

Chef's Note
- Rosamarina is better known as orzo, which is rice-shaped pasta that is often used for soups.

GRILLED CHICKEN SANDWICHES

Boneless skinless chicken breasts dry out on the grill, often shrinking into hockey-puck results. And that's not summery at all! So brine the breasts first — that way, they're plump and moist right off the grate.

1 small onion, sliced
3 bay leaves
4 (6- to 8-oz.) boneless skinless chicken breasts
3 cups water
¼ cup salt, preferably sea salt or kosher (coarse) salt
2 tablespoons honey
10 black peppercorns, crushed
Vegetable oil for grill grate
1 beefsteak tomato, cut into 4 slices
1 small red onion, thickly sliced
8 large thick-cut slices white or country white bread
1 large ripe avocado, peeled, pitted and sliced
1 cup bean, garlic or radish sprouts
Mayonnaise, mustard or bottled vinaigrette to taste, for garnish

1 Place onion and bay leaves in medium baking dish. Lay chicken breasts on top. In medium bowl, whisk water and salt until salt dissolves; whisk in honey and peppercorns. Pour over chicken breasts. Cover; refrigerate at least 2 hours but no more than 6 hours, turning breasts occasionally without disturbing onions.

2 Heat grill for direct cooking. Remove chicken from marinade; discard marinade. Pat chicken dry with paper towels. Let stand at room temperature while grill heats.

3 Brush grill grate with oil. Place breasts on gas grill directly over high heat or on charcoal grill 4 to 6 inches directly over high-heat coals. Grill, turning once, 11 to 13 minutes or until meat thermometer inserted into thickest part of breast registers 160°F for medium (preferred doneness) or 180°F for well-done. Transfer to carving board; let rest 5 minutes. Maintain grill temperature.

4 Brush grill grate with oil again. Place tomato and red onion slices over high heat; grill, turning once, 3 minutes or until browned and soft. Transfer to carving board; set aside.

5 Place bread slices on grill over high heat. Toast, turning once, 1 minute or until brown. Transfer to carving board. Slice chicken into strips, if desired. Assemble sandwiches on bread with chicken strips, tomato slices, red onion slices, sliced avocado, sprouts and mayonnaise, mustard or bottled vinaigrette.

Serves 4.
Preparation time: 25 minutes.
Ready to serve: 2 hours, 45 minutes.
Per serving: 510 calories, 18.5 g total fat (3.5 g saturated fat), 95 mg cholesterol, 2190 mg sodium, 5.5 g fiber.

SOUVLAKI

All across Manhattan, people line up for Souvlaki at stands, which are simply grills set up on street corners. You can make this Manhattan lunch favorite for your next backyard barbecue. Tell your guests you got the idea from a guy at the corner of 48th and 6th.

½ cup olive oil
¼ cup lemon juice
4 garlic cloves, crushed
2 teaspoons chopped fresh oregano
1½ teaspoons salt
½ teaspoon freshly ground pepper
1½ lb. lamb loin, cut into ¾-inch cubes
2 cups yogurt (regular, low-fat or nonfat)
1 small cucumber, peeled, seeded and shredded
2 teaspoons chopped fresh dill
4 metal skewers or 4 (12-inch) bamboo skewers, soaked in water 20 minutes, then drained
6 pita pockets
Shredded lettuce, diced tomatoes and thinly sliced red onions, for garnish

1 In large bowl, whisk olive oil, lemon juice, 2 of the garlic cloves, oregano, 1 teaspoon of the salt and pepper until well combined. Add lamb cubes; toss to coat. Cover; refrigerate at least 1 hour but no more than 3 hours.

2 Heat grill for direct cooking. Bring lamb and its marinade back to room temperature while grill heats.

3 Meanwhile, in medium bowl, mix yogurt, cucumber, dill, remaining 2 garlic cloves and remaining ½ teaspoon salt. Dressing can be made in advance — refrigerate, covered, up to 3 days.

4 Thread marinated lamb cubes onto skewers. (Do not blot lamb dry.) Fit as many cubes as you please on skewers without crowding — this is only to aid grilling, not for presentation. Place lamb skewers on gas grill directly over high heat or on charcoal grill 4 to 6 inches directly over high-heat coals. Cover; grill, turning once, about 8 minutes or until meat thermometer inserted in middle cube on 1 skewer registers 160°F for medium or 170°F for well-done.

5 Build Souvlaki by placing grilled lamb cubes and dressing in pita pockets; top with lettuce, tomato and red onion, as desired.

Serves 6.
Preparation time: 1 hour, 30 minutes.
Ready to serve: 1 hour, 40 minutes.
Per serving: 450 calories, 20.5 g total fat (6 g saturated fat), 90 mg cholesterol, 735 mg sodium, 2 g fiber.

GRILLED SCALLOPS WITH YELLOW PEPPER RELISH

Scallops on the grill are done in minutes; their natural sweetness caramelizes over high heat. Marinate them in oil first so they don't dry out.

Scallops
24   large sea scallops (about 1½ lb.), cleaned*
2   tablespoons olive oil
1   teaspoon salt
½   teaspoon freshly ground pepper

Yellow Pepper Relish
2   yellow bell peppers, cut into quarters
1   small onion
4   cups boiling water
½   cup lukewarm water
½   cup plus 2 tablespoons white vinegar
3   tablespoons sugar
¼   teaspoon salt
¼   teaspoon crushed red pepper

Variations
Herbed Grilled Scallops

- You can also skewer scallops on herbs. Rosemary and thyme sprigs work especially well. For each scallop, remove half the leaves from a 4- to 5-inch sprig; whittle the rosemary sprigs to make a thin, arrow-like point. Just before grilling, insert 1 sprig into each scallop, piercing it from side to side (not top to bottom).

- You can also lay 1 basil leaf on top of each scallop just after it's gone onto the grill rack. In this case, do not turn the scallops but let them gently steam 5 minutes under the basil.

1   Heat grill for direct cooking.

2   **For Scallops:** Place scallops in large resealable plastic bag; pour in olive oil, 1 teaspoon salt and ground pepper. Seal bag; toss gently to coat. Set aside at room temperature to marinate 10 minutes.

3   Place scallops on gas grill directly over medium heat or on charcoal grill 4 to 6 inches directly over medium-hot coals. Grill, turning once, 4 to 5 minutes or until scallops are opaque and barely firm to the touch.

4   **For Relish:** Shred bell peppers and onion. Place in large bowl; cover with boiling water. Let stand 5 minutes; drain.

5   In medium saucepan, bring bell pepper mixture, lukewarm water and ½ cup of the vinegar to a simmer over high heat. Remove from heat, cover. Let stand 10 minutes; drain.

6   Return pepper mixture to saucepan. Stir in remaining 2 tablespoons vinegar, sugar, ¼ teaspoon salt and crushed red pepper. Bring to a simmer over medium-high heat. Reduce heat to low; simmer 10 minutes or until thickened, stirring often. Relish can be prepared ahead. Store, covered, in refrigerator up to 1 week.

Serves 4.
Preparation time: 10 minutes.
Ready to serve: 25 minutes.
Per serving: 220 calories, 8 g total fat (1 g saturated fat), 30 mg cholesterol, 965 mg sodium, 1 g fiber.

Cooking Tip
* On scallops, slice off the small muscle that arcs over one side of the meat.

PEACH MELBA

Peach Melba gets its name from 19th century opera singer Nellie Melba. This version adds baked meringues for extra crunch and texture. *Peach Melba* is packed with summer's goodness.

Vanilla Ice Cream
1½ cups milk
1 cup heavy cream
4 egg yolks
½ cup sugar
1 teaspoon vanilla

Meringue Shells
2 egg whites
¼ teaspoon cream of tartar
6 tablespoons sugar
2 tablespoons powdered sugar

Raspberry Sauce
1½ cups raspberries, fresh or frozen and thawed
½ cup raspberry jam
1 tablespoon Kirsch or orange juice

Peaches
6 peach halves, canned in juice, drained
6 tablespoons Kirsch (optional)

1 In medium saucepan, heat milk and ½ cup of the cream over medium heat until scalded.

2 Meanwhile, in medium bowl, whisk together egg yolks and ½ cup sugar. Slowly whisk ¾ cup of scalded milk mixture into yolks; whisk back into pan. Cook, stirring constantly over medium heat, until mixture thickens slightly and coats back of spoon. Immediately pour into clean bowl; stir in vanilla. Refrigerate, covered, about 4 hours to age. Whip remaining ½ cup cream to soft peaks; fold into chilled custard. Freeze in ice cream maker according to manufacturer's directions. Remove to chilled container; cover. Freeze 4 to 5 hours to ripen and firm.

3 Meanwhile, heat oven to 200°F. Line baking sheet with parchment paper. In medium bowl, beat egg whites at high speed until frothy; beat in cream of tartar. Continue beating to almost stiff peaks; beat in 2 tablespoons of the sugar and powdered sugar. Beat until stiff peaks form. Sprinkle with remaining 4 tablespoons sugar; fold into whites. Immediately spoon whites into 6 mounds on baking sheet. Using back of spoon, flatten slightly and form hollow in center. Bake 2 hours; turn off heat. Let cool in oven 30 minutes. Remove.

4 **To make sauce:** In blender or food processor, puree raspberries, jam and 1 tablespoon Kirsch. Strain to remove seeds. If desired, in medium bowl toss peach halves with 6 tablespoons Kirsch; marinate about 30 minutes. To serve, place 1 peach half, hollow-side up, in center of each meringue; add scoop of ice cream. Top with raspberry sauce.

Sertves 6.
Preparation time: 1 hour, 30 minutes.
Ready to serve: 9 hours.
Per serving: 445 calories, 17 g total fat (9.5 g saturated fat), 190 mg cholesterol, 80 mg sodium, 2 g fiber.

GRILLED STONE FRUIT WITH CHOCOLATE SAUCE

Grilling fruit intensifies its flavor. This is also a great way to use the heat of dying coals left over from a summer cookout. Enjoy this dessert outside, admiring the sunset or watching the stars twinkle.

6   ripe apricots, halved, pitted
6   ripe peaches, preferably white, halved, pitted
6   ripe nectarines, halved, pitted
6   oz. bittersweet chocolate, preferably Scharfen Berger, chopped
3   tablespoons half-and-half
2   tablespoons framboise (optional)
1   cup fresh red raspberries

1 Heat grill.

2 Fill bottom of double boiler half full with water; bring to a boil over medium heat. Reduce heat to low so water simmers slowly.

3 Arrange apricots, peaches and nectarines skin-side down on grill rack 4 to 6 inches from medium hot coals. Cook until fruit begins to soften and brown, about 3 to 5 minutes.

4 Arrange fruit, skin-side down, on serving platter; cover with tea towel to keep hot.

5 Set top part of double boiler on top of simmering water; add chocolate and half-and-half. When chocolate is melted, stir gently to mix. Slowly add framboise, if using.

6 Drizzle chocolate sauce over fruit; garnish with raspberries. Serve immediately.

Serves 6.
Preparation time: 30 minutes.
Ready to serve: 35 minutes.
Per serving: 285 calories, 14 g total fat (7.5 g saturated fat), 5 mg cholesterol, 5 mg sodium, 9 g fiber.

NEW S'MORES

Use the coals remaining from your barbecue dinner to toast the marshmallows for this camp favorite. One warning: A barbecue grill is big and very hot. This dessert isn't kid-friendly — you'll need to make it for them. But the kids just might have to wrestle these s'mores away from the adults! Double or triple this recipe at will. You might need to.

8	whole graham crackers
1	(4-oz.) thin white chocolate bar, cut into 4 pieces
12	large marshmallows
¼	cup chopped macadamia nuts
1	(4-oz.) thin dark chocolate bar, cut into 4 pieces

1 Remove grill grate. Heat grill for direct cooking.

2 Lay 4 graham crackers round-side down on work surface. Top each with 1 piece white chocolate.

3 Push marshmallows on ends of each skewer or wooden stick. If using skewers, wear grilling gloves or use heavy-duty hot pads. Toast marshmallows over low heat or low-heat coals about 3 minutes or until browned.

4 Using fork to remove hot marshmallows from skewers, place 3 on top of each white chocolate piece. Sprinkle hot marshmallows with 1 tablespoon nuts. Top each with 1 piece dark chocolate, then graham cracker, pressing gently to create sandwich. Allow marshmallows' heat to soften chocolate, about 1 minute. Other topping ideas include: almond or cashew butter, apple or pear butter, jam, jarred caramel sauce, jelly, marmalade, nutella, peanut butter, and preserves.

Serves 4.
Preparation time: 15 minutes.
Ready to serve: 20 minutes.
Per serving: 515 calories, 25 g total fat (11.5 g saturated fat), 5 mg cholesterol, 195 mg sodium, 2.5 g fiber.

PEACH-BLACKBERRY COMPOTE WITH BASIL SYRUP

There is a secret ingredient in this sophisticated summer fruit compote: fresh basil, which has a special affinity with peaches. The basil garnish is a clue to the subtle — yet distinctive — flavor in the syrup.

¼   cup sugar
3   tablespoons dry white wine
3   fresh basil sprigs
2   (2-inch) strips orange peel (thin colored portion only)
3   cups sliced peeled peaches (1½ lb.)*
1   cup fresh blackberries, rinsed
1   tablespoon fresh lemon juice
    Fresh basil sprigs

1. In small saucepan, simmer sugar and wine over medium heat. Remove from heat; stir in 3 basil sprigs and orange peel. Cover and steep 30 minutes.

2. Strain syrup into small bowl, pressing on basil and orange peel to release flavor.

3. In large bowl, combine peaches, blackberries and lemon juice. Add basil-infused syrup; toss gently to coat. Garnish with basil sprigs.

Serves 4 (1-cup servings).
Preparation time: 20 minutes.
Ready to serve: 50 minutes.
Per serving: 125 calories, 0.5 g total fat (0 g saturated fat), 0 mg cholesterol, 0 mg sodium, 4.5 g fiber.

Cooking Tip
* To peel peaches, dip them into boiling water for a few seconds, and then slip off the skin.

HOMEMADE MASCARPONE ICE CREAM WITH AMARETTO-PLUM SAUCE

Mascarpone is a soft, cream-based cheese from Italy. It is much richer and softer than our regular domestic cream cheese, and it brings a unique flavor to one of the most interesting ice creams you'll ever create or taste. *Amaretto-Plum Sauce* makes the perfect summer topping.

Mascarpone Ice Cream
- 2 cups half-and-half
- 1 (8-oz.) carton mascarpone
- ½ vanilla bean, split lengthwise
- 5 egg yolks
- ⅔ cup sugar

Amaretto-Plum Sauce
- 3 firm-ripe plums, pitted, sliced
- 1 (10-oz.) jar plum jam
- ¼ cup almond flavored liqueur (or ¼ cup water and ¾ teaspoon almond extract)

1 In medium bowl, whisk ¼ cup of the half-and-half into mascarpone to soften; set aside. Place remaining 1¾ cups half-and-half in medium saucepan. Scrape seeds from vanilla bean into half-and-half; add pods. Heat over medium heat until scalded; remove from heat. Allow to steep 10 minutes. Remove pods.

2 Meanwhile, in medium bowl, whisk together egg yolks and sugar. Whisk ½ of scalded cream slowly into egg yolks; whisk back into pan. Cook, stirring constantly, over medium heat until mixture thickens slightly and coats back of spoon. Do not boil. Immediately pour into clean bowl. Cool to room temperature; whisk into mascarpone mixture. Freeze in ice cream maker according to manufacturer's directions. Remove to chilled container; cover and freeze 4 to 5 hours or overnight to firm and ripen.

3 Before serving, place plums, jam and liqueur in medium saucepan. Melt jam over medium-low heat, stirring often to combine and prevent scorching. When melted, reduce heat to low; continue cooking 5 minutes, stirring occasionally to soften plums slightly. Remove from heat; let cool slightly. Scoop ice cream into individual serving bowls. Spoon Amaretto-Plum Sauce over.

Serves 6 to 8 (About 4 cups ice cream).
Preparation time: 30 minutes.
Ready to serve: 6 hours.
Per serving: 400 calories, 20.5 g total fat (11.5 g saturated fat), 185 mg cholesterol, 125 mg sodium, .5 g fiber.

SPARKLING MINT LIMEADE

For pure warm weather refreshment, nothing beats homemade limeade or lemonade. In this version, the citrus base is infused with herbs and diluted with sparkling water for a lively finish.

1   cup fresh mint sprigs, plus more for garnish
1¼ cups fresh lime juice
⅔   cup sugar
    Ice cubes
3   cups (750 ml) chilled sparkling seltzer or
      soda water

1 In medium bowl, bruise mint with pestle or wooden spoon to release fragrance. Add lime juice and sugar; stir to dissolve sugar. Cover and refrigerate at least 2 hours or up to 8 hours.

2 Strain lime juice mixture, pressing on mint sprigs to extract flavor. To serve, place several ice cubes in each of 4 tall glasses. Pour ⅓ cup lime juice mixture into each glass; top off with ¾ cup sparkling water. Garnish each serving with a mint sprig.

Serves 4 (1-cup servings).
Preparation time: 20 minutes.
Ready to serve: 2 hours, 20 minutes.
Per serving: 145 calories, 0 g total fat (0 g saturated fat), 0 mg cholesterol, 55 mg sodium, 0.5 g fiber.

Chef's Notes

- To make lemonade, substitute rosemary sprigs for mint, lemon juice for lime juice, and reduce sugar to ½ cup. Garnish with rosemary sprigs.
- Whether you're serving lemonade or limeade, dip the edge of each glass in honey, then sugar.

S U M M E R

CRAFTS

Summer is beautiful. With flowers blooming and a full bonanza of other great natural materials available, some of the year's best crafting happens when the weather is at its warmest. Armed with all the ideas and instructions in this chapter, you'll be able to create craft projects that really celebrate summer and all the good things this most beautiful of seasons has to offer.

Facing page: Fruit and Vegetable Wire Basket, page 64

NOTES FROM A GARDENER

In this hectic era of cell phones and instant messaging, it's a special treat to receive a hand-written note. When impassioned gardener Mary MacDonald sends a note, her friends know it wasn't dashed off and hurriedly deleted from the to-do list. Her notes are not only handwritten but hand-made too, using pressed flowers from her garden. Here's how.

A few dabs of Elmer's household glue hold the pressed flowers permanently in place on the card. The time-consuming part is at the front end. It takes a while to learn which flowers hold their color and which fade, which have the most striking patterns, which stand up to pressing, and which fall apart or just crumble away to nothing.

To press the flowers, you can use a professional flower press, but MacDonald prefers phone books. She always has five or six phone books filled with flowers, which means that whenever the urge strikes to send a note to a friend, the raw materials are ready and waiting, all year round.

After two or three weeks in a phone book, many flowers are even more lovely in their paper-thin state than fresh-picked because the colors are more subtle and luminous, and the lines of petal and leaf are more pronounced.

MacDonald's favorite flower for pressing is the tulip. For leafy designs she says ferns make the most eye-catching patterns. Other blooms that press well are poppies, pansies, hibiscus, clematis, dahlias, and many wildflowers. Blue flowers tend to lose their color, but try them anyway, she says. They may surprise you.

1 If you're using flowers from the garden, pick them at midday when the flowers are dry. You can pull large, fleshy flowers apart. If they have fat centers (like tulips), press only their petals.

2 Place the flowers and/or leaves between the pages of a phone book. Use a phone book from a medium-sized city (under a half-million population); its directory is small enough to be flipped through quickly. Place a 50-pound weight on top of the phone book and wait two to three weeks.

3 Select blooms and apply to the card, using a small dab of white glue with a toothpick. (You don't need much!)

Materials & Tools

- Fresh flowers
- Medium-sized phone book
- 50-pound weight (a pair of 25-pound hand weights, bricks, cement blocks, a cast-iron doorstop, or similar objects)
- White note cards (card stock available from paper-supply stores)
- Elmer's household glue
- Toothpicks for applying the glue

Pressed Flowers in a Double Glass Frame

There are many ways to decorate with pressed flowers. This is a simply adorable way to preserve a piece of your garden to display all year long. The double glass frame enhances the translucent quality of thin colored petals. Selecting a thoughtful color palette and flower arrangement offers you an opportunity to express your creativity.

Materials & Tools

- Approximately five to ten pressed flowers (either hand-pressed or store-bought)
- Two pieces of glass or plexiglass, 5 inch by 5 inch
- Aluminum foil tape (at least ½ inch wide)
- Scissors
- Bone folder
- Craft tweezers

Craft Tips

- Bone folder can be purchased at craft or stamping stores.
- Set glass frame on easel for a pretty display.

1 Arrange the pressed flowers on the backing piece of glass using craft tweezers to avoid fingerprints.

2 Place the second piece of glass on top.

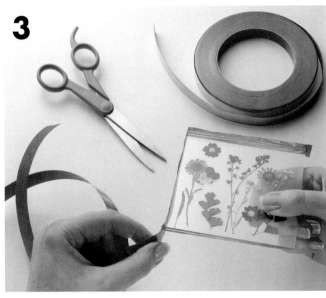

3 Evenly apply the foil tape around the two pieces of glass.

4 Cut the excess tape with scissors. Press the tape onto the glass using a bone folder to create a tight seal.

EASY MOSAIC POTS

Nothing sets off a lovely plant like a decorative pot. But pots can be expensive. With a little bit of effort and some chipped or broken pottery, excess tile, marbles or polished rocks, you can transform your plain-Jane pots from boring to beautiful. And once you've experimented with an easy mosaic design on a clay pot, you're ready to tackle just about any surface that needs a face-lift. Be creative! Try a tabletop (pictured), a flea-market picture frame or even a backsplash.

Materials & Tools

- Unglazed clay pot
- Marker
- Tiles, plates, pottery, stones, marbles, etc., for mosaic pattern
- Plastic knife or flat stick
- Premixed adhesive/grout (available in various colors at home-supply centers)
- Paper or burlap bag
- Protective eyewear
- Hammer
- Sponge
- Grout float (optional)

1 Draw your design on the clay pot (Photo 1). The larger the surface area, the larger and more intricate your design can be, depending on your imagination, expertise and patience.

2 Place tiles, plates or other mosaic materials inside a paper or burlap bag (Photo 2). Put on protective eyewear. Using a hammer, break the mosaic materials into small, workable pieces. If some pieces still seem too large, break them in the bag again.

3 Spread premixed adhesive/grout onto a small area of the pot. Begin placing the broken mosaic pieces onto your design on the pot (Photo 3). Keep working this way until the entire pot is covered. Allow the pot to dry overnight.

4 Now you're ready to grout the pot. You can use a grout float (available at home-supply centers) or a plastic knife to press the premixed grout into the voids between the tiles. Let stand for about 15 minutes.

5 Use a moist sponge to wipe off the excess grout. You may have to wipe down the surface multiple times to get it clean. Let dry overnight.

Craft Tips

- Using premixed adhesive/grout will eliminate mixing. Also the "glue" will be the same color as the grout and you won't have to worry about the adhesive showing through where you don't want it to.
- When applying the pieces to your mosaic, apply only enough adhesive/grout to cover an area that can be worked in about 15 minutes. The adhesive may dry too quickly if you try to cover a bigger area than you can work.
- The more intricate your design, the smaller the mosaic pieces need to be. If your design is intricate, it may be best to dry-fit an area with the mosaic pieces, then adhere each piece individually.
- Be patient. The surface will look much better when it is grouted.
- Mosaics take time; a really complex pattern can become tedious to work with. Be patient.

GARLIC AND RED PEPPER BRAID

This garlic and red pepper braid will add an organic touch to your kitchen. Garden vegetables evoke warm thoughts of summer harvests and gourmet cooking. Its natural aesthetic is an inviting complement to any home. This decoration is guaranteed to be appreciated by garlic lovers.

- Eight bulbs dried garlic
- 25 dried red peppers
- Jute twine
- Scissors

1-2

1 Cut three pieces of 48-inch-long twine.

2 Fold them in half and tie them together near the top of the loops. Braid the twine and tie the ends.

3 Cut 18 pieces of 8-inch-long twine. Tie a piece of twine around the top of each garlic bulb. Start filling the braid by pushing the top of the first bulb through a section at the bottom of the braid. Tie the garlic onto the braid. Cut the excess twine. Attach each piece of garlic alternating from the left to the right side.

3

4

4 Tie twine around a group of three red peppers. Then tie the peppers to the braid filling in the empty spaces between the garlic bulbs. Trim the excess twine.

Craft Tip

- Because garlic and peppers are dried, they should last a year or two.

WHIMSICAL BIRDFEEDER

Garden art is always a hot home trend. Statues, birdbaths, fountains, birdfeeders … you name it. There are many wonderful items of outdoor decor to create.

It's easy to see why garden art is so popular: Colorful shapes help brighten otherwise dull landscapes. This easy birdfeeder project is a perfect way to add a little form and function to your own yard.

To complete this project, you need a bamboo birdcage. Bamboo birdcages once held small birds such as parakeets, and were a popular indoor decorating staple. Today, you'll often find them available at tag and estate sales fairly inexpensively. (These two cost $10 and $15, respectively.) You may even find such a cage tucked away in your own attic, too pretty to throw, but too impractical to use as is.

Better yet, because this project involves adding structural strength to the birdcage as part of the "retro-fitting" process, your cages don't need to be in perfect shape. You can use birdcages that are slightly damaged, as long as you take care to reinforce weak spots with either wire or wooden supports.

1 Place the birdcage on a table or other platform where you can easily reach all sides. If the feeder is dusty or dirty, use a dry paintbrush to clean off the cage before starting. Slide out the removable cage bottom so that you can reach inside the cage as you begin to wire.

2 To add stability to your birdfeeder, you will need to reinforce all of the junctions where the walls meet. This includes the spots where the roof meets the walls, and all corners.

Snip off several inches of wire, and carefully weave it through the bamboo sticks at a corner, curling the wire around adjacent sticks on a separate wall. Continue to weave and tie the wire at that spot until only an inch or two remains. Using the needlenose pliers, twist both ends of the wire together, and clip off excess wire. Bend under the knotted portion of the wire so that no rough edges stick out. Repeat this process with additional wire at each corner of the cage.

3 After reinforcing each corner, set the cage upright. Locate the birdcage door. Use craft paint to outline a section of adjoining bamboo pieces about 5 inches tall by 6 inches wide. (This will help you see which pieces of bamboo you will cut out next.)

4 Removing some portions of the bamboo walls allows small birds to enter and exit the feeder easily.

Set the birdcage on its side. Put on safety goggles, and use tin snips to cut each piece of painted bamboo just above and below the nearest horizontal wall supports. Remove all painted bamboo sections to create an opening in the side of the cage.

(Note: In most old bamboo birdcages, each thin bamboo stick runs from the bottom support up through several additional supports, and ends at a final support in the roof of the cage. When you cut these sections in the middle, the bamboo will tend to slip down from the top. Don't worry about this. Simply slide the sticks back in place. You will reinforce them in the next step.)

5 After you have removed the bamboo sections, measure the width of the opening in the birdcage. Cut two of the craft or popsicle sticks to size to fit within the hole, one for the top support, and one for the bottom.

If your craft sticks are particularly wide, use a sharp utility knife to split them lengthwise.

6 Cover one side of craft stick with wood glue. Place the stick within the birdcage opening, holding it in place with your fingers until the glue has a chance to bond. Once the glue has set, further secure the support by wrapping with additional wire. Repeat this step at both the top and bottom of each opening. (It's easier to place the top support stick first, and then to set the cage upright and place the bottom stick in place.)

7 Repeat steps 4 through 6 on each side of the feeder. If the birdcage has more than one "story," create additional openings on each level.

Set the cage aside until the wood glue has dried thoroughly (overnight is best). Once dry, spray paint the birdcage in a bright color. (Set the cage in a large cardboard box outside, and spray one side of the cage at a time. The box will keep the paint from accumulating on your grass.)

Once the cage is painted, seal it with a coat of clear varnish. Place a flat bowl to hold birdseed on the birdcage bottom, and slide bottom back in place.

Hang the cage outside and enjoy!

SUMMER SHOW-OFF

This summer, add a colorful accent to entryways, patios, fences, arbors and even trees with the cascading blooms of a hanging moss basket. As you plan your moss basket, carefully consider the basket's location—sun, shade or partial shade—because it determines plant choices and the amount of watering needed. Additionally, protect your baskets from the hot midday sun and brisk, dry winds because hanging baskets dry out more quickly than other containers.

For a sunny location, try geranium, marigold, petunia, moss rose (*portulaca*), ageratum, verbena, vinca, sweet potato vine, ivy, alyssum, zinnia, dusty miller, dianthus or licorice plant (*helichrysum*). For part shade and shade, use pansy, violet, impatiens, coleus, fuchsia, Mexican heather, bacopa, begonia or lobelia. Choose young, smaller plants, which grow faster than older, larger ones.

When planning plant combinations, the choices of texture, shape, height and color are limitless—be creative! Consider a variety of annuals, vines, herbs or even vegetables. For example, attract butterflies with marigolds, nasturtiums and lantana. Grow a garden salad of lettuce, parsley, cilantro, chives and miniature tomatoes. Or entice passersby with the fragrance of thyme, rosemary, lavender, mint or oregano.

To spice up the basket, choose warm colors (red, orange, yellow); to ice it down, use cool ones (blue, green, violet). For night, think white—white heliotrope, flowering tobacco or white petunias. Complementary colors (yellow and purple, red and green, blue and orange) add lively interest. Or use related colors, such as purples and blues, or yellows and oranges, for a more unified effect. Varying shades of green foliage add dimension and depth.

Be sure to hang your moss basket where you can enjoy its color and fragrance—and where you can get to it easily, because you'll need to water it daily during hot weather. Remember to hang it from something sturdy because wet moss baskets get heavy.

Materials & Tools

- Hanging wire basket
- Sphagnum moss (not sphagnum peat moss)
- Plants (approx. 14 plants for a 14-inch-diameter basket)
- Potting soil (not garden soil)
- Fertilizer (if desired)
- Container of water
- Trowel
- Extra pot to support basket while working
- Strong, durable hook for hanging

1 Assemble the materials and soak moss in a container of water until saturated.

Craft Tips

For Long-Lasting, Glorious Color

- Water daily or as needed.
- Pinch off faded blooms.
- Fertilize as needed (follow fertilizer package instructions).

2 Line the inside of the basket with a 1- to 1½-inch layer of soaked moss. Working from bottom to top, push moss against wire form to create a solid nest (Photo 2).

3 With a trowel, make holes in the outside of the nest where you intend to add plants. Carefully insert root ball of plants through holes to the inside of the basket (Photo 3).

4 Add potting soil and fertilizer to the inside of the basket and position remaining plants at top of basket (Photo 4), grouping color and height combinations to best effect.

5 Water thoroughly, using a water wand for a gentle spray.

FRUIT AND VEGETABLE WIRE BASKET

Weaving with wire is a very creative and satisfying process. Wire can be bent and formed into any shape imaginable. A wire basket will keep those summer-ripened fruits and vegetables easily accessible. This item is attractive and practical for any home.

- 24-gauge spool of tinned copper wire
- 16-gauge spool of tinned copper wire
- 18-gauge spool of tinned copper wire
- Twisted 16-gauge wire
- Wire cutters
- Long-nosed pliers
- Flat-nosed pliers
- Paper
- Pencil

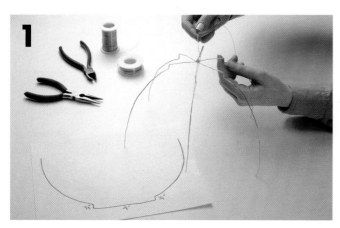

1 Draw an outline of the desired basket shape on a piece of paper. Bend three pieces of 16-gauge wire along an outline drawing for a basket. For this particular basket, the lengths of the three pieces of wire were 17½ inches. Use the pliers to bend the wire into the correct angles. Leave ½ inch of extra wire at each of the ends and then cut the excess wire. Next bend each piece of wire at the middle of the bottom at about a 45-degree angle. Tie the three pieces of wire together by wrapping 24-gauge wire around the corners of each bend. Tuck in the end of the wire.

2 Make the rim by shaping the twisted wire into a circle. This 9-inch-diameter basket required 27 inches of wire to make the rim. Bend a hook at each end using the long-nosed pliers. Crimp the two ends together. Attach the rim by making a hook at the end of each rib using the long-nosed pliers. Crimp each of the hooks around the rim.

3 Cut six pieces of 24-gauge wire about 1½ feet long. Hook and twist each piece of wire onto the bottom of each rib using the flat-nosed pliers to hold the spirals in place.

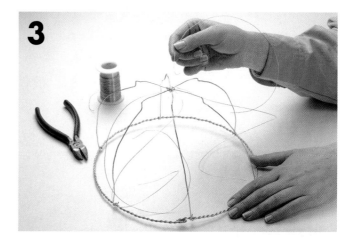

4 Make a hook and crimp 18-gauge wire onto the bottom of a rib. As you spiral the wire up the basket, wrap the 24-gauge wire twice around the rib and spiral wire, each time you pass a rib. Spiral the wire up to the rim, leaving a ¼ to ½ inch space between spirals. Hook and crimp the 18-gauge wire onto a rib. Cut the excess wire.

MOSAIC WINE BOTTLE COASTER

Share long summer evenings with dear friends and a favorite bottle of wine. This charming mosaic wine bottle coaster is eye-catching and protects your table linens from wine stains. This practical and stylish coaster is perfect for entertaining, or as a gift for the wine aficionado.

- Wood or fiber-board circle ½ inch thick with 5-inch diameter
- Vitreous glass tesserae
- Mirror
- Gem-Tac or similar permanent adhesive
- Grout, premixed, non-sanded
- Two-wheeled mosaic cutter
- Tile nippers
- Glass cutter
- Running pliers
- Ruler
- Rubber gloves
- Sponge
- Lint-free cloth

1 Cut each glass tessera into quartered squares with the two-wheeled mosaic cutter until you have approximately 50 pieces. Then cut the corners of each smaller square with tile nippers to create a circular shape.

2 Cut the mirror into strips using the glass cutter and a ruler as a guide. Break the strips off with running pliers. Next, cut the strips into approximately 50 squares with the two-wheeled mosaic cutter. Then cut the squares at each of the corners with tile nippers (same as the circular-shaped glass tesserae).

3 Apply each tile and mirror with permanent adhesive. Place them ⅛ inch apart or less.

4 Spread the grout onto the surface wearing rubber gloves. Remove the excess grout and wipe down the tiles with a damp sponge. Polish the tiles and mirrors with a lint-free cloth after the grout has dried.

Craft Tip

- Purchase specialty tools such as a two-wheeled mosaic cutter, tile nippers, glass cutter and running pliers at a glass materials and tools supplier.

EASY GARDEN BENCH

Rustic furniture is a natural for the garden because many of the materials used to construct it can be found right on site. An added advantage to building furniture out of twigs and branches is that you don't need to measure carefully or join parts precisely.

Of course, all the parts must eventually fit together, but don't worry if the end result is a little crooked; that will add to its charm. Infuse a bit of European character into this twig-built garden bench by joining the parts with dowels in a way that's similar to contemporary knockdown furniture. It's also a lot easier than the traditional mortise-and-tenon construction method. If you want to get into the true spirit of this rustic project, build it outdoors where it will reside.

Building Plan

The drawing below isn't meant to provide every construction detail, but to give you a sense of size and proportion. The dimensions are only approximate; this is a cut-and-fit project. For instance, pieces such as the short, curved braces should be cut long and trimmed after fastening. Typically, seat height is about 18 inches and seat depth is about 20 inches.

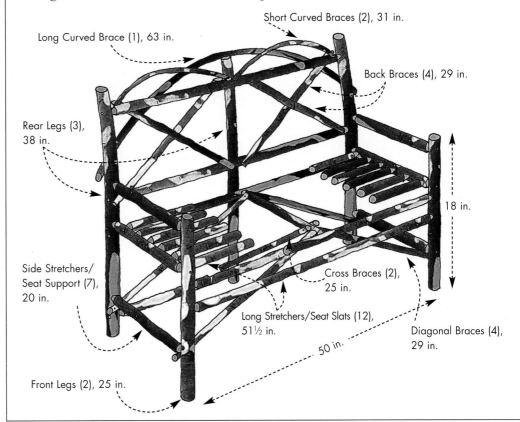

Short Curved Braces (2), 31 in.
Long Curved Brace (1), 63 in.
Back Braces (4), 29 in.
Rear Legs (3), 38 in.
18 in.
Side Stretchers/Seat Support (7), 20 in.
Cross Braces (2), 25 in.
Long Stretchers/Seat Slats (12), 51½ in.
Diagonal Braces (4), 29 in.
50 in.
Front Legs (2), 25 in.

Materials & Tools

Your biggest challenge will be finding straight branches that are somewhat uniform in shape and size. Good sources of materials include recently trimmed trees, community compost centers and nurseries. To work, the wood must be green—dry wood splits easily and won't bend well. Almost any tree or large shrub will work, and you can even mix different kinds. However, branches with smooth bark are more comfortable to sit on. (Avoid resinous trees such as pines.) For the rear legs, pick pieces with a natural crook so the back will angle out and improve stability. Use your imagination: Gnarled or twisted branches can add character. Just be sure to smooth the branches to avoid snags.

- A 2-foot by 4-foot piece of hardboard for pattern template (see photo 3).
- Use 1½-inch and 2½-inch diameter branches (approximate size) for the bench framework, and ¾-inch-diameter pieces for the curved parts and back braces (see drawing above).
- Use ¾-inch dowels for joining pieces.
- Use galvanized nails (10d is a good size) to pin the dowels and the places where pieces overlap.

- handsaw
- hammer
- chisel
- knife
- electric drill (a brace would work, too)
- ⅛- and ¾-inch spade drill bits.
- Hand plane, knife or chisel to smooth the branches.

1 Once you've selected the branches you need, cut off any protruding knots and twigs with a handsaw.

2 Smooth the cut areas with a hand plane, knife or chisel so they are flush. Always cut away from your body.

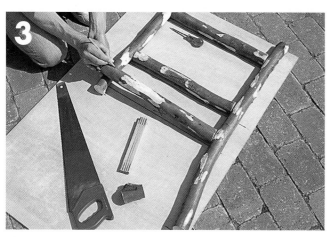

3 Draw a pattern for the arms, legs and sides on a piece of hardboard. Use this as a template to cut and fit pieces.

4 Drill small pilot holes in the arms and side stretchers; then use a ¾-inch spade drill bit to bore dowel holes.

5 Taper the ends of the pieces with a hammer and chisel. Use a knife to refine the points.

6 Bore the corresponding dowel holes for the arms and side stretchers in the front and rear legs.

7 After assembling the sides with dowels, bore ⅛-inch pilot holes for the reinforcing nails, then drive them into place.

8 Lay out the holes for the seat slats, seat-back stretchers and leg stretchers. Then bore about three-fourths of the way through the stock.

9 Assemble the bench by first inserting all the stretchers and slats into one side. Then attach the other side and nail.

10 Nail the middle leg, leg braces, back supports and bent braces. Use oversize pieces and trim once secure.

Craft Tips

- Although there's nothing wrong with gluing the joints (polyurethane glue is best), there's really no need. The green branches will transfer moisture to the dowels, causing them to swell and tighten the joints. As the branches dry, they'll shrink around the dowels and secure the joints even more.

- To keep the wood from splitting when nailing, bore ⅛-inch pilot holes before driving the nails. Where nails go completely through overlapped joints, such as the back braces, cinch the joint together by bending the nail point where it punches through.

- Seal the bottoms of the legs to prevent rot, but you don't need to seal the entire bench. Don't get hung up on trying to make this a permanent piece. Work quickly, have fun, and use wood that would otherwise be discarded.

LAVENDER SACHET

The aromatic scent of lavender uplifts the senses. Lavender-filled sachets add decorating style and pleasing fragrance anywhere you desire. In a lingerie drawer, the linen closet, or placed in the car, this inviting scent is naturally soothing. You can also try using miniature rosebuds for their sweet perfume, or any other favorite scent you choose.

1 Ink the lavender stamp with a stamping pen and press it onto the cotton cloth.

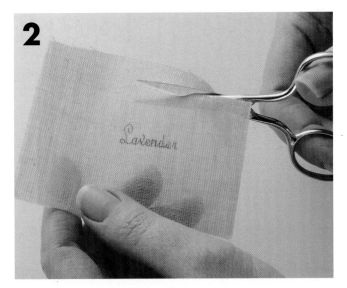

2 Cut out the stamped cloth in a rectangular shape to attach to the front of the bag. Before attaching the cloth, pull out a couple pieces of thread from each side to create fringes.

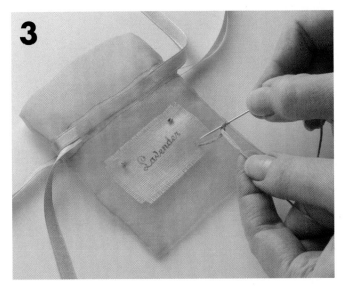

3 Sew the cotton cloth onto the bag with an "x" stitch at each corner with lavender embroidery thread.

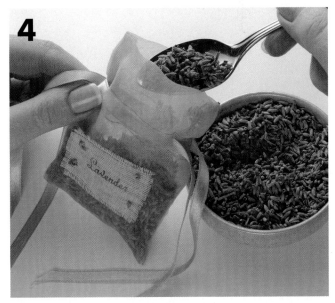

4 Fill the bag with lavender, and then tie the bag closed.

Materials & Tools

- Dried lavender, approximately ¼ cup per sachet
- Sachet bag
- Loose weave cotton cloth (such as linen)
- Lavender rubber stamp (of the name or illustration)
- Lavender stamping pen
- Lavender embroidery thread
- Needle
- Scissors

Craft Tips

- Try using a French knot to attach the corners of the cotten cloth to the sachet bag.
- A "Lavender" stamp can be purchased at an arts and crafts store.
- Use a fabric pen to hand write "Lavender" instead of using a rubber stamp.

FRAGRANT LAVENDER WAND

These wands are an easy and elegant way to add the soothing and summery scent of lavender to a room. Pretty enough to leave out on a table, you can also use these sachets in linen closets or drawers to gently perfume your favorite bedding or lingerie. These wands make practical sachets because the lavender flowers are encased in ribbon cages so they won't "sprinkle out" among your delicate things.

You can also leave the wands out on a shelf in the bathroom, where the color and patterns will delight the eye and, as a bonus, you will enjoy their delicate scent whenever the room gets steamy.

These wands last for a long, long time. To renew their scent after a few months, gently squeeze the wand to release more of the aromatic oils from the lavender.

To refresh the wands even further, add a couple of drops of essential lavender oil to the stems to keep the fragrance intact for years.

Lavender wands are easy to make. Give them a try. The project becomes even more rewarding when you grow your own raw materials (see below).

Materials & Tools

- Scissors
- Four yards $\frac{1}{8}$- to $\frac{1}{4}$-inch ribbon
- Fresh lavender with long stems (35 stems per wand as shown)

Do It Yourself
Grow Your Own Lavender

There are hundreds of varieties of lavender with colors ranging from white, pink and pale lilac to darkest purple. The varieties of *Lavandula* x *intermedia*, like "Provence," "Grosso" or "Grappenhall," bloom on 30- to 40-inch stems, so these varieties are perfect for making lavender wands.

When lavender is planted in the herb garden or in the perennial border, bees buzz around the fragrant flowers and small butterflies will alight in evening to drink the nectar. Lavender blooms for up to three weeks during summer, but cut lavender also can be used as a dried flower, culinary herb or fresh flower indoors.

Cut lavender when the buds are just starting to show color. The petals will unfurl from the tiny buds and last up to two weeks in sparkling clean water.

Lavender generally is not used in traditional flower arrangements because a few stems get lost among more showy blooms. Display fresh lavender in informal bunches in several small containers. Below, a gardener has stuffed handfuls into pink pots to accompany wild sweet peas.

1 Cut off 24 inches of ribbon and set aside. You will use this ribbon in the last step. Run your fingers down each stem of fresh lavender to strip off all the leaves. For this wand, we used 35 individual stems of lavender.

2 Carefully bunch all the lavender stems together. Use one end of the large piece of ribbon to tie a knot just under the blossoms, leaving the rest of the ribbon dangling.

3 You will be weaving the ribbon in and out among groups of stems. You must divide your stems into an uneven number of groups. (I started with 35 stems and divided them into seven groups of five stems each.) Grasp 5 stems near each other and gently bend them down over the flowers. Take the ribbon at the knot and place over this group. Now bend down another group of five and weave the ribbon under. This start is the only tricky part of making the wand.

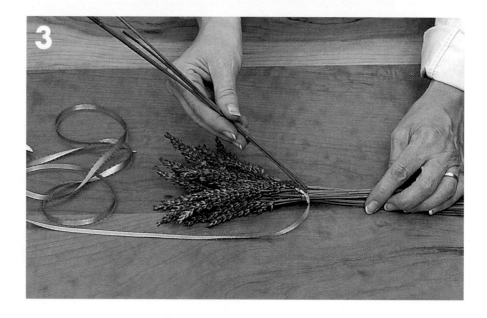

4 Continue bending down the rest of the stems in groups of five, weaving the ribbon under and over each group. Because you have an uneven number of groups, you can keep weaving over and under in a regular pattern until you have formed a nice checkered pattern with the ribbon and have completely encased the flowers in a woven cage.

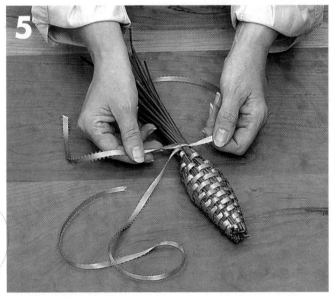

5 Tie the wand at the base of the weaving with the reserved 24-inch piece of ribbon. Tie the woven piece into the bow as well for a third streamer.

6 Trim the ends of the ribbon and the ends of the stems. Leave the wand in a warm, dark, dry spot, and the wand will dry in about a week. Once dry, place in a drawer or display as desired.

Craft Tips

- To make bigger or smaller wands, start with more or fewer stems. But the total number of stems must always divide into an uneven number of groups. If you want a bigger wand, you could use 49 stems divided into 7 groups of 7 stems each. For a small wand, use 15 stems split into 5 groups of 3 stems each. Naturally, the length of ribbon needed will vary with the size of your bunch.

- Be sure to make the wand within a day of cutting or buying your fresh lavender so that the stems won't break as you bend them to form the cage.

ROSE QUILT

The concept of quilting inspired this design. If you admire both contemporary and traditional patterns but can't seem to find the time or patience to produce those neat and tiny stitches, here's a fun and beautiful alternative. Granted, this rose quilt won't keep you warm in winter, but you can display it as a piece of art reminiscent of summer. Hang your rose quilt on a wall, place it on a mantel, or prop it in a stand on a side table.

To make this quilt, select a shadow box frame that is square or rectangular, or have one made to your dimensions at a frame shop. Order one to your specifications so you can get the color, size and style you need for a particular project. For a wedding gift, match the colors to the preferences of the couple. A custom frame will not cost much more than a ready-made, unless you choose something elaborate. Take the time to select a pleasing mat color, because you may decide to have some of the mat visible as part of the design.

The amount of materials needed will, of course, depend on the size of the frame and how many squares you are making.

Materials & Tools

- A variety of colors and sizes of roses, rose leaves or other flowers and herbs (see Craft Tip below for alternate suggestions)
- Silica gel
- Dust mask
- Airtight container
- Scissors or floral shears
- Flower press or heavy phone book
- Square or rectangular shadow box frame
- Acid-free mat board, also called museum board
- Ruler
- Pencil
- Hot-glue gun and glue sticks

Craft Tips

- Dried flowers hold their color best if they are displayed away from direct sunlight in an environment with low humidity. For example, avoid a bathroom, which gets a lot of steam, and any location near a window. Sealing the finished quilt under glass in a shadow box will also help preserve the colors. The best tip of all is to start with strong colors. No wimpy pastel pinks, no pale yellows and no creams. The orange-red of the Mercedes or Tropicana roses is very long-lasting.

- The quilt presented here, with roses and leaves only, looks equally spectacular with other dried flowers and herbs from your garden or a floral shop. As with sewn quilts, your design is limited only by your imagination and your materials. Give your quilt another name or a theme and you'll immediately know what you need. For a patriotic quilt, use reds of cockscomb and roses; whites of straw flowers, pearly everlasting, feverfew and money plant (*Lunaria*); and blues of globe thistle, delphinium, bachelor button or blue statice. To complement modern decor, opt for hot colors: the golds of perennial sunflower (*Heliopsis*) and yarrow, bright purples and hot pinks of statice and globe amaranth, and reds of cockscomb and small dried hot peppers.

1 Before beginning this project, you will need to dry the fresh flowers you have selected. As an option, if your time is limited or if you're in a hurry to begin, you can purchase air-dried or freeze-dried roses from a craft or hobby shop, and skip to Step 6.

You can air-dry roses by hanging them upside down in small bunches in a warm, dark, dry spot. However, for a better appearance, I prefer to dry my flowers in silica gel, a sand-like substance that pulls water from the flowers. To use silica gel, first put on a dust mask, and then carefully pour a 1-inch layer of the material in the bottom of an airtight container. Set the container aside for the moment.

2 Completely snip off the stems of your fresh roses, leaving only the swelling at the base of the flower. Snip off the leaves and set aside (see Step 5).

3 Stand each rose upright in the silica gel, positioning them so that they are close but not touching.

4 Pour the remaining silica gel gently around the flowers until they are completely buried under another inch of the material. Cover the container, and leave undisturbed for two weeks. At that point, you can pour off the silica gel and save to reuse. (I've used mine for 14 years, hence the little flecks of past projects that are visible in the sand.)

Shake all the silica off the roses and set the dried flowers aside.

5 While you wait for your roses to dry in the silica, press the leaves that came off the roses in a flower press or heavy phone book. When the flowers are ready, the leaves will also be ready.

6 To prepare the frame, measure the mat and block into squares, making light pencil marks. Here, the measurement of the mat is 15½ by 15½ inches. I left ¼ inch of the mat on all sides, which will be hidden under the frame. The finished size of the quilt will be 15 by 15 inches, divided into nine squares of 5 by 5 inches.

7 Visualize the placement of your flowers and leaves. Plan ahead. Set your materials where you think they should go, before gluing. Make any necessary changes, then glue in place.

Craft Tip

• Start on the inside of your design and work out to the edges, gluing as you go.

S U M M E R

DECORATING

S ummer offers natural beauty outside. It's easy to bring that feeling indoors and incorporate it into your decorating scheme. All you need is a little time, not very many dollars, and the decorating ideas in this chapter. These projects were designed for success on your part, so dive right in. And remember. You'll be creating the look and feel of summer ... but you might just decide to display the feeling all year 'round in your home.

Facing page: Summer Wonder Wreath, page 92

WOODEN FLOWER BOX

Weathered wood and birdhouse detail makes this flower box unique. Great for a porch with flowers or a kitchen counter with herbs, this box will hold three 3-inch clay pots or 4-inch (usually measuring about 3½ inches) plastic pots. This way you can purchase plants and put them directly into the box without transplanting.

This project is great for a novice woodworker because it does not have to be perfect and needs no sanding. Irregularities exist in weathered wood such as nail holes, warping and varying thickness. This is what gives it character and charm.

The weathered board used here is about 8 inches wide and 1 inch thick. If the boards are not as thick, adjustments need to be made for the length of the 1¾-inch side panels. Try to avoid using fresh-cut edges in areas that will be seen. This window box can be made of new cedar or pine and would look best in ½-inch lumber. Painting the pine is recommended.

Materials & Tools

- Weathered board, 8 inch by 1 inch, by at least 36 inches
- Finishing nails in 1½ inch and 1 inch
- Table or radial saw
- Drill with small bit for starting nail holes and ¾-inch bit for "birdhouse" hole

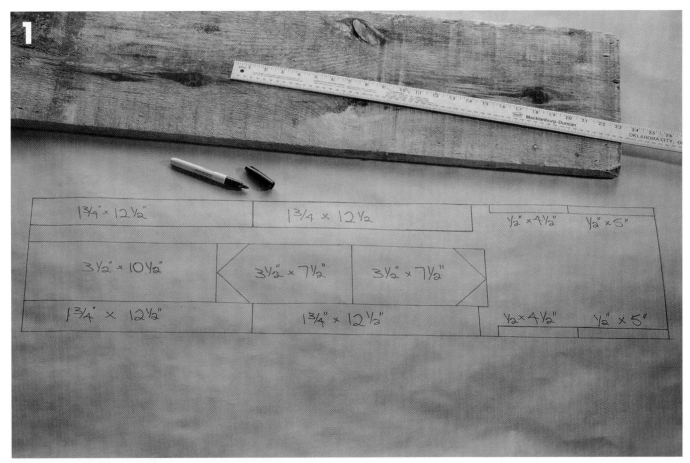

1 Cut the following pieces according to layout to be able to use weathered edges as much as possible:

- Bottom – 3½ inches by 10½ inches.

- Sides – 4 pieces, each 1¾ inches by 12½ inches.

- Ends – 2 pieces, each 3½ inches by 7½ inches, cut to a 45 degree point at one end.

- Roof – 2 pieces, each ½ inch deep by 4½ inches; and 2 pieces, cut ½ inch by 5 inches.

2 Drill a ¾-inch hole in end piece about 4 inches up from bottom and centered.

3 Always use drill to make pilot holes for nails to prevent splitting and make pounding the nails easier. First place one end piece at one end of bottom piece, drill 2 holes and nail together. Do the same for opposite end. Place one side piece at bottom, lining it up with ends. Secure with two nails at each end. Space next side piece (weathered edge showing) about 1 inch above bottom piece. Secure these in the same way. Do opposite side.

4 Place 4½-inch roof piece even with top edge of roof and secure with 1-inch nail. Use 5-inch roof piece for other half of roof and overlap at top to make roof come to a point. Secure with 1-inch nail. Do opposite side.

Craft Tip

- Use a scrap of wood from project to hold top side piece in place. It should be about 1 inch thick.

SUMMER MEMORIES TABLE RUNNER

Summer is full of opportunities for taking the year's best pictures. But why hide them away in an album? Instead, turn them into a fun and personalized table runner!

Most families take more pictures in the summer than any other time of the year. Plus, there are certainly pictures from summers past, still floating around here or there or in boxes. What better way to enjoy all this photographic bounty than by displaying them all over the table?

Although it isn't necessary, the best place to do this project is at a scrapbooking store. Most scrapbooking stores have a work area where you can really spread your project out on a table. You can use their die-cut machines and specialty edging scissors at no charge if you buy your paper there. Brainstorm with the papers in front of you, and buy only what you are actually going to use. It's also fun to see what everyone else is working on. If you haven't yet discovered the fun you can have with old, repeat or unused photos, this project will be an inspiring introduction.

Materials & Tools

- Black-and-white photocopies of your favorite pictures
- Four 8½- by 11-inch sheets of black card-stock paper
- Various sheets of "specialty paper" (various colors with designs printed on them)
- Tape
- Glue stick
- Scissors (Fiskars Paper Edgers, if available)
- Flower and bug stickers
- Die-cut cutouts (available precut at some craft stores)
- Laminating, available at local copy center

1 Gather pictures you want to use. If you don't want to cut up actual photos, make black-and-white or color copies.

2 Tape four pieces of black card-stock paper together, side to side, to form the base of the runner. Cut a 3-inch border out of one of the specialty papers and tape it, on the underside, to the card-stock paper runner.

Craft Tips

- You can copy pictures for only cents apiece in a regular copier. You can enlarge the pictures 200% by setting the image option to "photo." Ask for help if you need it! If you prefer to use color copies, you will pay a lot more, but you will treasure the end result more as well.
- This table runner makes a great gift for Grandma and Grandpa!

3 Cut out the pictures (using Fiskars Paper Edgers, if available). Using the glue stick, glue the picture onto the specialty paper, and cut around the picture, creating a ¼-inch border around the picture.

4 Arrange the pictures on the runner, and when you are satisfied with the placement, glue them down. Add die-cut cutouts and stickers.

5 Take the runner to a copy store and have them laminate it for you. Cut away excess lamination plastic, leaving about ¼ inch extra around all edges.

Variation

Create personalized placemats, with pictures of each member of the family, for their own spot at the table.

FLORAL SPECIES DISPLAY

Display the variety of flowers you have growing in your garden. Floral identification enriches our appreciation for many varieties of flowers. Playfully scientific, this method of display is attractive and educational. Others will naturally enjoy learning to identify flora while admiring your flowers.

Materials & Tools

- Wooden test tube rack
- Wood stain
- Five 16 mm glass test tubes
- Glass-frosting spray

- Self-adhesive paper
- Small pebbles
- Lint-free cotton rag
- Craft knife

- Marker
- Pencil

1 Purchase a wooden rack from a scientific laboratory supplier or online, or build one from scratch.

2 Stain the wooden rack with a lint-free cotton rag.

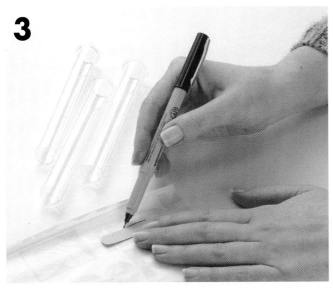

3 Draw and cut out templates using self-adhesive paper for the glass tube's frosted label. The label should be approximately 10 mm wide and 47 mm long.

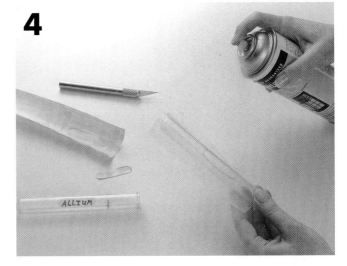

4 Adhere the mask to a tube and spray with glass-frosting spray. Be careful not to spray any other part of the tube.

5 Write the name of each flower using a marker on the frosted label. (Scientific names can be found on the internet or in a gardener's reference book.) Drop a small amount of pebbles into each tube. Fill with water and flowers.

SUMMER WONDER WREATH

Wreaths aren't just for the holidays anymore. In fact, you can make one of the most beautiful and inviting wreaths of all, using summer's beauty!

Most of us have a fascination with and appreciation of nature, especially what is so close by in our own backyards. In the winter, maybe birds, squirrels and chipmunks visit to enjoy black sunflower seeds and homemade suet. But in the summer, the yard is filled with all kinds of winged wonders: colorful butterflies of many sizes nectaring on garden flowers, dragonflies flying around a pond or sunning themselves on a branch, and birds making nests under eaves and in birdhouses.

Whether you're gardening or just relaxing outside, try to spend many hours enjoying ALL the wildlife your backyard attracts (well, except for the mosquitoes). This delightful little indoor wreath celebrates all those summer wonders!

1 To begin your wreath, hot glue down the clay pots, bird's nest and strawberries. Glue in the artificial flowers. (Hint: If you keep the stems long on your flowers, you can insert them into the grapevine branches for extra stability.)

Materials & Tools

- 12 inch grapevine wreath
- Hot glue gun
- Two 3-inch-tall clay pots
- Artificial flowers
- Artificial strawberries
- Spanish moss
- Sheet or floral moss
- Artificial butterflies, dragonfly, bees, grasshopper, ladybugs
- Small artificial bird's nest, bird's eggs, and small bird
- 20-gauge floral wire

2 Separate the sheet or floral moss (green moss) into smaller pieces, and begin hot gluing it around the clay pots, bird's nest and strawberries. Hot-glue the Spanish moss (the grayish moss) on the outer edges of the sheet moss, and in the clay pots. Glue a little Spanish moss into the bird's nest, before gluing in the eggs.

3 Glue down the bird in her nest, the dragonfly on a grapevine branch, the grasshopper on a branch and the ladybugs crawling around on leaves.

4 To make the butterflies and bees appear as if they are flying around the wreath, cut a long piece of floral wire, about 10 inches in length. Make a small loop at each end of the wire, and twist the wire together. Wrap the wire around a pencil, creating a spiral.

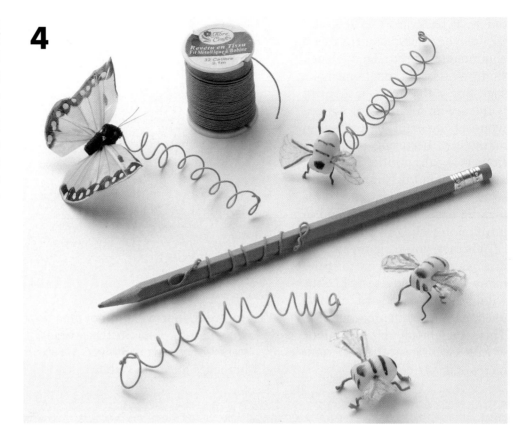

5 Hot-glue one end of the spiral wire to the undersides of the butterflies and bees. When the glue is cool, hot-glue the other end into the wreath. Position the butterflies and bees at angles and heights that make them appear as if they are flying around the wreath.

FLORAL DOOR TOPPER

Create this cheerful door topper to shout a colorful "Welcome!" to all your summer guests.

Summer is the perfect time to put a little more color and whimsy into your decorating, whether it's in the fun dishware you use on your picnic table, or in the playful way you decorate your home for the summer season.

Summer is also a time to relax and enjoy yourself, and here is a project designed to remind you to do just that — in a colorful and whimsical way!

This indoor floral door topper can be used in your kitchen, your bedroom or above an entry door that is protected from weather from above ... anywhere you need to be reminded to "stop and smell the flowers!"

Of course, you can also use your imagination and creativity to create your own welcoming phrase for summer.

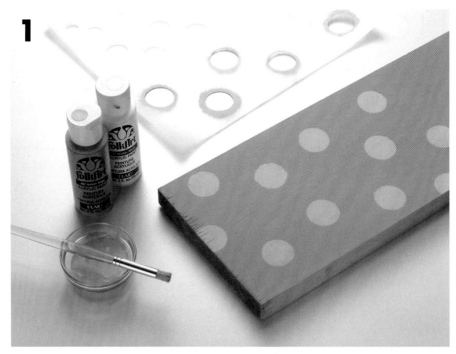

1 Paint the plywood board in sage green, and add a second coat if desired. When the board is completely dry, stencil polka dots over the entire surface. (Add a bit of sage green paint to the white paint if you would like to tone down the background polka dots.)

Materials & Tools

- A plywood board, new or old, measuring approximately 6 inches by 34 inches
- Picture hanger hardware
- Acrylic paint, sage green and white
- Paintbrush
- Polka-dot stencil (other options: checkerboard or stripes)
- Stencil brush
- Clear acrylic spray coating (found near the spray paint in stores)
- Large silk or paper flowers
- Wire cutters
- Glue gun
- Staple gun

2 Depending on which method you decide to use to make the letters (see page 97), stencil or glue on the saying: Stop and smell the flowers! When the paint or glue is dry, spray the board with a clear acrylic sealer. When the sealer is completely dry, nail on the picture hanger hardware to the back center of the top of the board.

3 With a wire cutter, cut away all but about 3 inches of the stem of the flowers. Remove the leaves from the discarded stems to use later. Place the flowers where you like them on the top of the board. Using your hot glue gun, glue the stem onto the back top of the board. When the glue is cool, staple over the stem for extra support.

4 With the hot-glue gun, glue down the extra leaves and any petals that are hanging close to the wood for extra strength. Hang your door topper above a door and enjoy.

Craft Tips

Making the Letters: Three Options

- **Stencil** — Depending on their width, use 1½-inch-tall (or so) letters. For this option, you will need an alphabet stencil, a stencil brush, tape (to hold the stencil in place) and black acrylic paint. Make a sample of the saying on paper to make sure the saying will fit on your board and to help to center it, before you begin stenciling.

- **Printout** — If you are computer savvy, find a font you like, enlarge the saying to fit your board, and print the saying in black on white card-stock paper. Cut the letters out and adhere them to the board using MOD PODGE or white glue. After the letters are cut out, you may want to paint over them with black acrylic paint, or go over them with a permanent black marker.

- **Stickers** — If you have a scrapbooking store near you, buy an alphabet template. Simply trace around the letters on black card stock, cut them out, and adhere them to the board using MOD PODGE or white glue.

SPONGED LADYBUG PLACEMATS AND NAPKINS

Sponging a design creates a porous and fun image, making these summery placemats and napkins great for picnics … or in making an indoor lunch seem like a picnic. The ladybug pattern is easy to make freehand. Each ladybug will look unique, since the sponged image will depend on amount and thickness of paint, as well as added features such as dots, antennae and legs.

The four placemats and coordinating napkins are easy to sew. Choose a mediumweight fabric that is 100 percent cotton or predominantly cotton, with a bit of a texture. Wash fabric to remove sizing and to shrink it. To care for the finished project, wash in cool water, delicate cycle. You may spray the completed project with a fabric protectant to help shed stains. If sewing is not an option, purchase the placemats and napkins. Wash them before sponging.

Sponging

1 On paper, sketch a slight oval about 1¾ inches long for the body. Sketch a circle about ¾ inch in diameter for head. Transfer to the compressed sponge by tracing around the patterns. Cut out both pieces and cut oval in half lengthwise and cut circle in half. (One half of circle will not be needed.) Place sponge pieces in water to expand. Let them dry a bit. This will take awhile. When sponges are almost dry, place a piece of corrugated cardboard between the two oval pieces. This creates the space between the wings. The piece of cardboard should be the length of the body and not as deep as the sponge thickness. With tape that is narrower than thickness of sponge, tape around the outside of sponge so body becomes one piece. Cut out paper patterns of ladybug body to use in deciding placement of designs. Designs should be placed at least 1¾ inches from edge of fabric to allow for adding legs, antennae and hem. Mark final design placement with fabric marker using about four dots placed around design.

2 Pour red textile paint onto a paper plate, spreading it into a circle about the size of the ladybug body. Sponge can be dampened a bit on the surface that will be used for paint. Place sponge in paint gently, so not a lot of paint is on the sponge. Check this by sponging on paper plate. Then gently but firmly place on fabric. Place some extra pressure around edges, and then remove. Let each ladybug body dry before adding other parts of design. The drying time should be about ½ hour.

Materials & Tools

Sponging

- Compressed sponge (can be purchased in craft store in the sponging/paint section)
- Textile paints in red and black
- Permanent fine-point paint pen in black
- Old chopsticks with round ends
- Paper plates
- Narrow masking tape

3

Materials & Tools

Placemats and Napkins
- 1 yard for placemats (Fabric A)
- 2 yards for lining of placemats and napkins (Fabric B)
- Matching thread

1

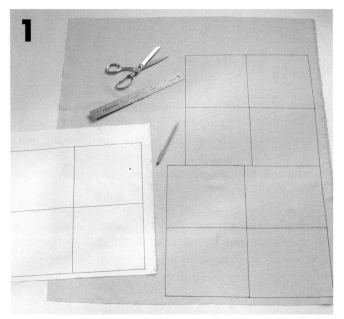

3 For the head, use black textile paint. Since the sponge for the head is small, use the paint jar lid to hold the paint. Place sponge in paint, as above, and place on ladybug design. Add spots by using the tip of a chopstick in black paint. Let dry. Using the paint pencil, add antennae and legs as shown in the photo. Let dry. Remove any fabric marker, with a bit of water sponged on mark.

4 Painted designs must be heat-set to make them permanent. Do this by pressing with an iron on the wrong side of fabric. Set the iron to the hottest setting appropriate for the fabric and hold 30 seconds or as directed on textile paint. Placemats and napkins are ready to be sewn.

1 Zigzag or serge around raw edges to prevent fraying. Wash fabric and press. Do not use selvages. Lay out four placemats on Fabric A, with width of placemat along the crosswise grain. Mark placemats to measure 15 inches by 17 inches. This will make a finished size of 14 inches by 16 inches. They may be a bit smaller or larger, if desired. Cut. On Fabric B, lay out lining for placemats, as above, and napkins to measure 15 inches square. Mark and cut. This will make finished napkins 14 inches square. They may be bigger, if desired. Keep extra fabric for practicing the sponged designs. *Now is the time to do the ladybug sponging (steps 1-4 on page 99 and this page).*

Craft Tip
- Before sponging the final project, practice any design on the extra fabric saved.

2 When sponging design is complete, make placemats by placing right sides together using sponged piece and lining Fabric B. Pin and stitch around edges with a ½-inch seam allowance, leaving a 3-inch opening at bottom edge of placemat for turning. Trim point off corners. Trim one corner closer to stitching. Do not trim closer than ⅛ inch.

3 Turn placemat right sides out, pushing corners out to square them. Make sure seam is at edge and press. Topstitching will secure opening that was left for turning. Topstitch first row about ⅛ inch from the edge. Second row of top-stitching should be about ⅛ inch from first row.

4 For the placemats, make a double turned hem by first turning a scant ¼ inch to wrong side and pressing. Then turn another ¼ inch to wrong side and press. Miter corners, by clipping off corner across first fold line and folding across second fold line. Stitch from wrong side close to folded edge.

STAMPED SEASHELL PICTURE FRAME

It's easy to make a special frame commemorating a special summer or seashore vacation. All you really need is a purchased stamp and a wooden picture frame.

The picture frame needs to have a flat surface of 1- to 1½-inch width for the stamped design. Making the design a bit random, and the amount of paint irregular, gives the best results.

It is easy to achieve varied color from light to dark on each stamped design. If an unfinished frame is used, more paint will be absorbed into the surface, which gives a different look. You can also seal the unfinished frame with a sand-sealer before doing the stamping. To use old wood frames, sand them down before starting the project.

Seashells are just one theme you can use for this lovely frame. Use any image that makes you happy!

Materials & Tools

- Picture frame
- Seashell (or other) stamp
- Craft acrylic paints in the following colors: turquoise, teal, blue, lavender, mauve and maroon or any other combinations you desire
- Clear acrylic sealer spray
- Paper plates
- Artist's brush
- Old toothbrush

Craft Tips

- A grocery bag works well. Try different placements and colors with your stamp.

- Put your chosen paint colors on a paper plate. The dollops of paint may be placed close enough to one another to blend. After experimenting, decide on your final design and colors.

- Use side of brush instead of tip. It is okay for colors to overlap. Paint can also be painted lightly in streaks for a lighter look.

- If you are not happy with one of the designs, you can immediately wipe it off with a damp paper towel.

1 Prepare frame by sanding lightly if the frame is finished. The shine needs to be removed so paint does not sit on surface.

2 To plan your design, trace the exact size of surface of picture frame on heavy paper.

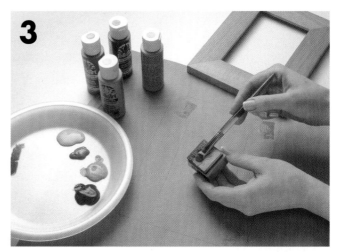

3 Use a paintbrush to blend paints (if desired) or paint very lightly one brush stroke of lighter color on the outside one-third of the stamp, another brush stroke of medium color in center and the dark brush stroke on the inside one-third of the stamp.

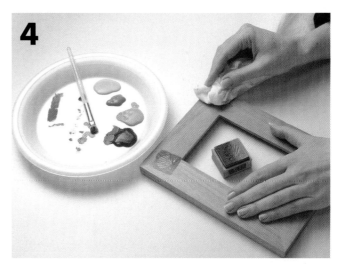

4 Press stamp onto frame firmly and remove. Use an old toothbrush to clean the stamp. Wash and dry stamp and brush between each use to prevent paint buildup and mixing of paint. Continue stamping designs until finished. Let dry.

5 Finish frame with two or more applications of clear acrylic sealer and let dry.

FLORAL MIRROR

It's common to use a mirror as a focal point of, or at least an accent for, a room's decor.

But it's uncommon to turn that mirror into a piece of art. Here's how!

Look for miniature paper and silk flowers in the bridal department of a craft store. When you add a beautiful wired ribbon (which looks antique by itself), this project appears as though it could have been handed down from great-grandmother. Hang this sweet little mirror just about anywhere. It's as beautiful as it is functional.

1 Twist and turn the wired ribbon and tap down with your hand to flatten it. When you like the look, hot-glue the ribbon around the outer edges of the mirror.

2 At the point where the ribbon begins and ends, glue two full paper roses, then continue gluing the paper rosebuds and miniature silk flowers down toward the middle of the mirror. Cut off the excess wire and stems of the little floral bundles to make it easier to tuck and glue the flowers under each other. Add extra leaves where needed.

3 With the excess wired ribbon, make a bow for the top of the mirror, and hot-glue it in place above the full roses.

4 Cut three lengths of thin green ribbon, 2 yards each. Hold the ribbon together, fold in half, and make a slip knot at the top, for a hanger. Hot-glue the green ribbon to the back of the mirror.

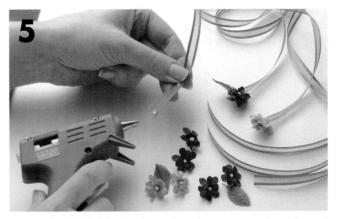

5 Embellish the slip knot by gluing extra leaves and flowers, and for a delightful finish, glue little flowers on the bottoms of the green ribbons.

STENCILED SUNSHINE FABRIC LAMPSHADE

Custom decorated lampshades add nice detail to any room or porch. You can match a theme or fabric with the stenciling you do. Here, the sunshine design is stenciled on white or off-white fabric cut to fit the lampshade.

Purchase lampshades in basic sizes and shapes at craft or fabric stores. An existing lampshade may be used if it is plain and clean, with a smooth finish. The instructions below are for an 8-inch flare shape. But you may need to make a pattern from your own shade, as the amount of flare may differ. The amount of flare will also affect the amount of fabric needed.

Practice the stenciling process on excess fabric. Purchase medium lightweight fabric in a plain weave fabric without texture or slubs. Wash fabric before starting this project; this makes it fit taut over the shade upon completion for the most professional look.

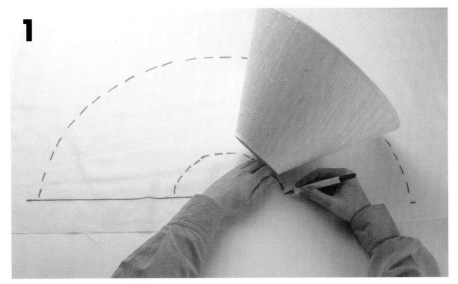

1 With a removable fabric marker, draw a line near the edge of the lampshade fabric. Align the seam of the lampshade to this line. Roll shade along fabric marking top and bottom until you get around to the seam. Mark a dot at the top and bottom of the seam. Add ½ inch seam allowance at seam. Add roughly an inch to top and bottom. Cut out. Keep extra fabric to practice stenciling.

Spread out single layer of fabric and place pattern at one straight edge of fabric. Smooth out pattern and secure to fabric with pins. Cut. Zigzag or serge edges to protect them from fraying. Keep extra fabric to practice stenciling.

2 Use shade outline, stencil and pencil to decide placement of stencil design. Measure around the lampshade about 1 inch above lower edge of shade. As an example, the above shade measured 30 inches, so designs were centered every 5 inches and 1¾ inches above lower edge line. Place first design about 1 inch from where seam will be stitched. Mark placement with fabric marker on cut fabric by using 4 dots, top, bottom and both sides.

Materials & Tools

- 8-inch lampshade
- 1 yard or less of fabric, plain weave in white or off-white muslin
- Sun stencil with a diameter of 2-3 inches
- Textile paint in a golden yellow color
- Small stencil brush, about ³⁄₁₆-inch width
- Masking and transparent tape
- White craft glue
- Matching thread
- Paper plates
- Fabric marker
- Pinch clothespins

3 Practice stenciling on extra fabric before working on final project. Place fabric on smooth surface that can be cleaned easily. Pull fabric taut and tape with masking tape. Place stencil over marked area and tape. Pour a small amount of yellow textile paint on paper plate. Using stencil brush with a small amount of paint, dab firmly, covering fabric within sun rays of stencil. In center circle, use a circular motion around edges and then toward the middle. Leave some areas bare or with varying thickness of paint to give more interest. Continue doing remaining designs. Clean stencil if paint builds up. Let dry, about 20 minutes.

Remove placement marks by dabbing with water. Heat-set paint by pressing on wrong side of fabric with hot iron for about 30 seconds or as directed on textile paint.

4 Sew seam and remove all markings. Put fabric shade on lampshade, smoothing downward until the fabric fits well. Trim the top seam allowance to ¼ inch. Put a bead of glue along raw edge and fold to inside. Clip with clothespins, if necessary. Allow to dry. Smooth fabric toward lower edge, trim to ¼ inch. Glue in place as above. Spray with fabric protectant to protect shade from dust and dirt.

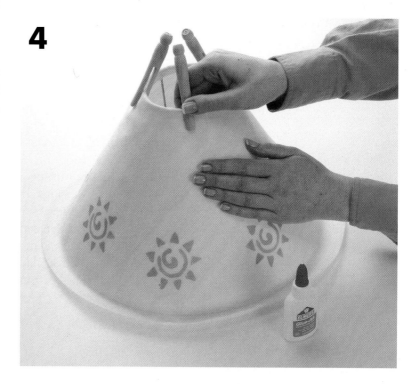

Craft Tips

- In addition to taping the stencil down, hold the stencil with your hand close to the area being stenciled. Pick the stencil straight up to prevent smudging.

- If excess stencil plastic overlaps the last design, trim off the excess plastic; otherwise, wait for each design to dry.

- The original seam allowed would have been ½ inch. But to get the appropriate taut fit, you may need to allow for a wider seam.

SOFT-SCULPTURE ROSE PILLOW

You don't need to be a sewing pro to create this lovely and decorative pillow. In fact, its beauty lies in its simplicity ... a short list of materials, and an easy process start to finish.

Polar fleece is the softest, most cuddly fabric available today. What better material for a pillow! A little girl would certainly enjoy this beautiful pillow in her bedroom, but so would the adults in the living room, so you may want to make more than one.

Polar fleece is also one of the easiest fabrics to work with. It goes through the sewing machine like a breeze, and is also easily manipulated to do the hand sewing required for this project. Best of all, it's machine washable so your pillow will be around for a long time to come.

Materials & Tools

- ½ yard burgundy polar fleece
- ¼ yard green polar fleece
- Polyester batting
- Burgundy and green thread
- Needle
- Sewing machine
- Scissors
- Pins

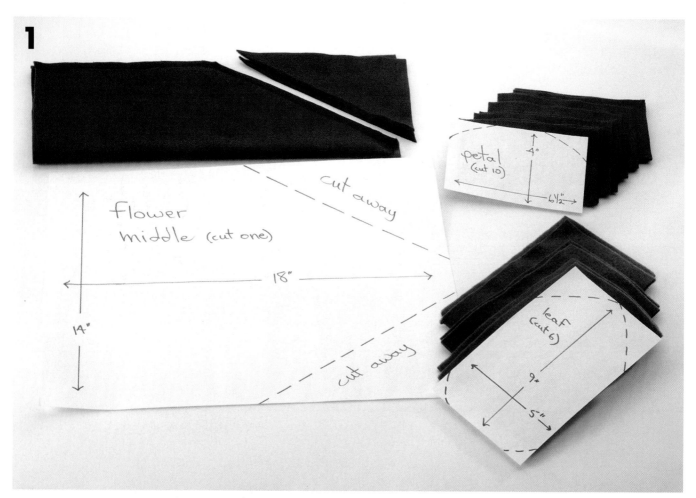

1 Cut out all the pattern pieces. With the right sides pinned together, sew the edges of the FLOWER MIDDLE together, leaving an opening on the large end. Turn the piece right side out. Stuff it with polyester batting, and hand-sew the large end closed, turning edges in about ½ inch.

- Flower – 14 inches by 18 inches.

- Petal – 10 pieces, each 4 inches by 6½ inches.

- Leaf – 6 pieces, each 9 inches by 5 inches.

Craft Tip

- Backstitch all seams for added strength.

2 To form the FLOWER MIDDLE: The large end of the FLOWER MIDDLE is the center of the rose. Wrap the long tail around itself so it forms a 'bud'. Hand-sew the end of the tail to the lower body of the bud. Hand-sew the very middle of the rose down to the bud so it is secure.

3 With the right sides pinned together, sew the edges of each FLOWER PETAL together, leaving an opening along the bottom edge. Turn the FLOWER PETALS right side out. Stuff each with polyester batting and machine-sew the bottom edge closed with a ¼-inch seam. Pin the FLOWER PETALS about 1 inch inside the bottom of the pillow, overlapping them slightly. Hand-sew them into place, and also hand-sew the middle of the FLOWER PETAL to a spot where it meets the FLOWER MIDDLE.

4 With the right sides pinned together, sew the LEAVES on the two long sides, leaving an opening at the bottom. Turn the leaves right side out. Lightly stuff the LEAVES with polyester batting. Hand-sew the bottom of the LEAF closed, turning under ¼ inch. Using green thread, machine-sew about 1 inch all around the inside of the LEAF surface, creating a more dimensional-looking LEAF. Position, then pin, the 3 LEAVES on the bottom of the pillow, making sure to cover your hand sewing. Hand-sew the LEAVES onto the bottom of the pillow, and hand-sew the middle of the LEAF to the bottom of the FLOWER PETALS.

SUMMER

GARDENING

Summer is the season for growing. Being outside in the garden ... working hard or just sort of puttering around and enjoying the day ... is one of life's greatest pleasures. But we all have gardening goals too, and these gardening ideas and projects can help get you there — from creating gorgeous color with flowers, to growing herbs for your cooking, to attracting lovely birds and butterflies, even making a mini pond.

Facing page: Bouquet Garden, page 118

BIRD AND BUTTERFLY GARDENS

One could hardly ask for better company in the garden than

colorful butterflies or chattering birds.

Both types of creatures will find your

garden irresistible if you do a few simple things

to make them feel welcome.

You can easily develop your landscape into an oasis for birds and butterflies by growing hospitable plants, providing a source of water and offering food when natural sources are in short supply. It is also essential to use no insecticides in a butterfly garden, and to avoid using fungicides and herbicides as much as possible.

Water and Food — Choosing the Right Spot

For a wildlife refuge, choose a spot that is warm and sunny during most of the day. Because butterflies are cold-blooded insects, they are most active in warm, sunny areas. Birds also like an open spot where they have a clear view of possible predators. Make sure you can see the wildlife area from inside your house on days when it's uncomfortably hot or cold outdoors.

Birds and butterflies share a common need for water. A shallow birdbath no more than 2½ inches deep with a few large flat stones placed in the bottom will meet the needs of both. Butterflies like to stand on a dry spot and sip water. Birds will use the same water for drinking, cleaning and raucous play. A broad, shallow watering dish placed on the ground also will work well as a birdbath. You might install a little pocket pond (see page 138) and add fish and frogs to your backyard wildlife brigade.

Try These

Choosing Plants for Birds

Look for areas where you can grow shrubs and small trees that give birds seasonal food and year-round shelter. The plants listed below are pretty enough to grow as specimen plants, or you can group them together to form a bird-friendly hedge or thicket. All produce flowers in spring followed by berries in the fall.

Small Trees
Dogwood (*Cornus florida*)

Ninebark (*Physocarpus* spp.)

Serviceberry (*Amelanchier arborea*)

Shrubs
Beautyberry (*Callicarpa americana*)

Juniper (*Juniperus* spp.)

Viburnum (*Viburnum* spp.)

Serviceberry (Amelanchier arborea).

Many viburnums are wonderfully fragrant.

Try These

Hosting Hummingbirds

Like butterflies, hummingbirds sip flower nectar. They will visit the same tubular flowers preferred by butterflies. You can supplement their diet by setting out hummingbird feeders in late spring. Planting red or bright orange flowers will also attract hummingbirds.

Fill hummingbird feeders with sugar syrup (one part sugar to four parts water), and clean them with hot water once a week. Between cleanings, don't worry if you find small insects floating in the feeder. Hummingbirds routinely consume small insects as they feed in flowers. To discourage bees and wasps, place a small amount of vegetable oil around the feeder's feeding holes.

Any red flowers will attract hummingbirds, and you can provide them with a feeder stocked with sugar water.

Good Plants for Hummingbirds
Cardinal flower (*Lobelia cardinalis*)

Honeysuckle (*Lonicera* spp.)

Hosta (*Hosta* cultivars)

Bee balm (*Monarda* cultivars)

Sage (*Salvia* spp.)

Red monarda or bee balm attracts hummingbirds and butterflies.

When hostas bloom, their tubular flowers host hummers.

Choosing Plants for Butterflies

Butterflies do most of their eating when they are caterpillars (their larval stage). The plants that the larvae eat, called host plants, include a few garden flowers but mostly weeds and wildflowers. Adult butterflies consume flower nectar from a wide range of flowers, which they sip through a long curling tongue-like organ called a proboscis. Because of the way they feed, flower form is more important to butterflies than flower color. Butterflies (and hummingbirds) flock to plants with short tubular flowers such as the aptly-named butterfly bush and butterfly weed. They also like flat, daisy-shaped flowers. Double blossoms crowded with petals make it more difficult for butterflies to feed, while single blossoms provide a platform for butterflies to stand upon while sipping flower nectar.

Keeping Butterflies Around

To keep butterflies happy all summer, use the seven butterfly favorites, listed at right, in your butterfly garden. Add other flowers both you and local butterflies find attractive. Butterfly populations are always highest in late summer, but they will remain with you well into fall if your garden includes autumnal bloomers such as asters, chrysanthemums, boltonia, sedum and goldenrod.

Monarch butterflies sip nectar from ornamental alliums. When they find a plentiful food source, it is not unusual for butterflies to feed in groups.

Garden Tip
Sensational Sunflowers

Expect to see plenty of bees on any sunflower during the first few days after the blossom opens. Three weeks later, as the seeds begin to ripen, finches and many other birds will promptly harvest them. Or you can cut the ripe old blossoms and save them for winter bird feeding. Sunflower seeds are ripe when the seeds fall out freely when you gently twist the dried flower. Also cut and save faded seedheads from the purple coneflowers you grow for butterflies. Birds love them!

'Park's Velvet Tapestry' sunflower.

Try These
Butterfly-Attracting Plants

Perennials
butterfly bush
garden phlox
purple coneflower

Annuals
cosmos
lantana
tithonia
zinnia

Purple coneflowers are fine butterfly plants.

Lantana.

Swallowtails find the tubular blooms of butterfly bush impossible to resist.

Butterfly Garden Site Selection

For a butterfly garden, select a site with the best solar access. Butterflies are cold-blooded and require warmth and sunshine. Morning shade is okay, as most butterflies are not active until around 10 a.m. and remain active into the early evening hours.

Make sure butterflies have places to bask in the sunshine. They bask with their wings perpendicular to the sun to gain enough warmth to live. Flowering plants also benefit from sunshine, and those that receive more sunshine will produce more nectar.

Situate butterfly gardens in locations protected from your region's prevailing winds. Butterflies gather in places that are a calm respite from the wind. Plant a windbreak of various shrubs and trees to block the wind. Install a fence or vine-covered trellis to break the wind in tight spaces or utilize your home or other buildings as a windbreak.

Locate butterfly gardens in areas where you can view and enjoy them as well. Butterfly gardens adjacent to outdoor patios and decks and outside family rooms, dining areas or dens are most enjoyable since those are locations where you, your family and guests spend the most time.

A sunny yard planted with prairie wildflowers and grasses creates an outstanding site for butterflies.

BOUQUET GARDEN

Cut flowers bring grace and beauty to indoor rooms, but there is another treat in store when you grow your own flowers for cutting. When you meet your flowers eye-to-eye, you will notice details about the blossoms that you may have missed in the garden—a refreshing new way to enjoy flowers, foliage and perhaps even weeds from your yard.

In arrangements, most flowers look best when they are at least twice as tall as the height of the container in which they are displayed. Short-stemmed pansies and nasturtiums are at home in small squat-shaped containers, but taller vessels call for long-stemmed flowers. Many varieties that develop long stems for cutting also are quite tall, so you may need to stake them as they approach their mature height.

Cut Flower Basics

You will need a spot of good soil that receives at least a half day of sun to grow select flowers for cutting. Some of the finest cut flowers to grow in your garden are described here, but you can use other plant materials from your yard in arrangements too. Foliage from evergreen shrubs, budding tree limbs, browned tops from wild grasses, even strappy leaves taken from iris or daylilies ... all enrich simple flower arrangements with their textures and forms.

Sunflowers and delphinium rest in water after being cut from the garden.

Color and Form

Flowers that work well with the colors in your indoor rooms make irresistible cut material. A bunch of a single type of flower always looks elegant when displayed in a glass container, but it's easy to mix and match flowers in unique arrangements. Here are two important guidelines for flower arranging success.

- Structure the composition with upright spikes that help define the arrangement's silhouette. Use branches and long-stemmed grasses. Spike-shaped flowers such as larkspur, veronica or plume-type celosias also work well for this job.

- Use plants that have neutral colors or soft textures to meld your composition together. Don't hold back when adding soft neutral plant material such as velvety gray dusty miller, sprays of baby's breath or rounded heads of Queen Anne's lace. Their textures will contrast beautifully with your feature flowers while giving your arrangements a full, lush look.

Larkspur, baby's breath, chrysanthemums and alliums anchor this softly hued cut flower arrangement.

Will They Drink?

The longest lasting cut flowers eagerly take up water through their cut stems. When experimenting with different flowers from your yard, watch to see if the water level in the vase drops overnight—a sure sign that the flowers are drinking their fill.

Handling Cut Flowers

To keep your stems looking fresh for days, take a container filled with water with you when you gather flowers. Remember to submerge the stems the moment they are cut and immediately bring the stems indoors, out of sun and warmth.

You must seal stems that bleed a white or clear sap after they are cut, to keep nutrients from escaping. Singe the bottom of the cut stems in a candle flame until they barely blacken, then return them to a container filled with water. Flowers that benefit from this treatment include butterfly weed, columbine, iris and poppies.

Flowers with hard or woody stems will take up water better if you use a sharp knife to make ½-inch-deep slits in the bottom of the stem. This treatment also works well with shrubs or bud-bearing branches gathered from flowering trees.

While it may seem a bit fussy, recutting the stems of cut flowers under water keeps an air bubble from forming (which blocks the transfer of water up the stem), and has a significant effect on the flowers' longevity.

Feature Flowers for Cutting

Chrysanthemums and dahlias are the dynamic duo among devotees of home-grown cut flowers. Both are easy to grow and will last in a vase for up to two weeks when properly handled.

- Garden chrysanthemums (which are different from florists' mums) are hardy perennials that bloom in late summer and fall. In Zones 3 to 5, try pink 'Clara Curtis' or yellow 'Mary Stoker', both of which are super hardy and dependable. Most midseason mums perform well in Zones 6 and 7. The midseason cultivar known as either 'Single Apricot' or 'Hillside Sheffield Pink' is outstanding in the garden and the vase, and the same is true of 'Yellow Jacket'. In Zones 8 and 9 you can grow late-blooming cultivars as well as special warm-natured strains that bloom twice a year, in spring and fall. Look for them at local nurseries. Dig and divide all mums every other spring, just after new green growth appears.

'Ginger' garden chrysanthemum.

Try These
Cut-and-Come-Again Annuals

Flowers that develop stem buds that grow into new flowering branches produce more flowers the more often they are cut. To make the most of this growth habit, cut stems just above a robust node—the place on the stem where new leaf buds can be clearly seen. No flower arranger should be without vigorous cut-and-come-again annuals such as these:

Celosia	Gomphrena
Salvia (*salvia farinacea*)	Snapdragon
Strawflower	Zinnia

The aptly named 'Cut-and-Come-Again' variety of zinnia produces new blossoms continuously over a period of two months or more.

- Dahlias are tender perennials that grow from tuberous roots. In Zones 7 to 9, leave them in the ground through winter if protected with a good mulch. In other zones, dig the tubers in late fall and store the cleaned roots in a cool, frost-free place until the following spring. Choose your dahlias based on color and flower form, and be sure to stake varieties that grow more than two feet tall. Grow dahlias in rich soil and full sun. Fertilize them in spring and midsummer.

'Border Princess' dahlia.

GROWING GOURMET HERBS

Herbs bring pleasure to the gardener with their interesting forms, fascinating history, folklore and wide range of fragrances. However, it is the flavor of herbs—what they do for foods—that makes them especially loved.

Herbs include annuals (basil, dill), perennials (chives, mint) or hardy biennials (parsley). Growth habit also varies from extremes such as low, ground-hugging thyme to tall, lanky dill. Herbs are grown mainly for their edible leaves, but some produce tasty flowers and seeds too.

Herbal Basics

Herbs are most often planted in their own separate area in the garden, frequently in formal raised beds where they benefit from improved drainage. You can also grow herbs in containers, in your vegetable garden, or tucked into flower beds. As long as herbs get plenty of sun and fertile, well-drained soil, they will likely thrive with little care.

No matter where you grow herbs, use them in all aspects of your cooking. Even though there are certain classic combinations, such as basil and tomatoes, there are no hard-and-fast rules as to what goes with what. Nibble on your herbs, finding the flavors you like best. Then consider which of your favorite foods they might enhance. The right herbs bring fresh flavors to pasta sauces, simple steamed vegetables, salad dressings, breads and many other foods.

A summer garden of herbs and flowers delights all your senses.

Rosemary comes in several different forms, such as this trailing variety. Expect a similar level of diversity with basil, mint and thyme.

Ten Top Culinary Herbs

- **Basil** (*Ocimum basilicum*) The most treasured annual herb of summer is a snap to grow as long as the weather is warm. Buy seedlings or start basil from seeds sown indoors four weeks before the last frost. Do not transplant outdoors until the weather has turned summery. Pinch out growing tips to encourage branching; remove flower buds to prolong a plant's life. There are dozens of types and varieties of basil and they are all wonderful.

Basil.

- **Chives** (*Allium schoenoprasum*) The thin, hollow green leaves of chives offer a delicate onion flavor. Growing in clumps, they produce leaves from early spring to late fall. Established plants bear edible mauve flowers in late spring. Hardy to Zone 3, start chives from seeds or grow from transplants. Divide clumps every two to three years to rejuvenate them.

Chives.

- **Cilantro** (*Coriandrum sativum*) Cilantro leaves are indispensable in Mexican and Southeast Asian cooking. Resembling flat-leaf parsley, cilantro leaves are best when picked young. A half-hardy annual, cilantro grows best in cool weather and quickly goes to seed. Cilantro does not transplant well, so sow seed directly into the garden monthly from spring until early fall.

Cilantro.

- **Dill** (*Anethum graveolens*) This easy annual is as pretty as it is edible. The ferny plants grow to 3 feet tall, and quickly produce round umbels of yellow flowers. Dill does not transplant well, so sow seed directly into the garden. Make successive plantings every 3 or 4 weeks for a continuous supply of fresh leaves. If allowed to develop mature seeds, dill will often reseed itself.

Dill.

- **Mint** (*Mentha* spp. and cultivars) This incredibly vigorous herb comes in a wide range of flavors, some with fruity overtones. A perennial hardy through Zone 4, mint tolerates light shade. Mints can be invasive and are often grown in pots to keep them from taking over the garden. Cut back plants after flowering to stimulate the growth of new stems.

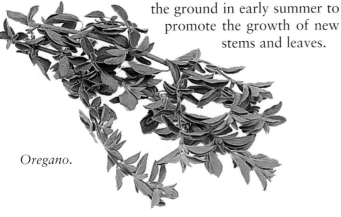

Mint.

- **Oregano** (*Origanum* spp. and cultivars) Synonymous with Italian food, oregano is a dependable perennial hardy through Zone 5. The bushy, spreading plants grow 1 to 2 feet tall, with small oval leaves and clusters of tiny purple or white edible flowers. Cut plants back almost to the ground in early summer to promote the growth of new stems and leaves.

Oregano.

- **Parsley** (*Petroselinum crispum*) Parsley comes in two forms, curly and flat. Curly parsley has finely divided and twisted leaves on 12-inch-tall plants. Flat-leaf or Italian parsley has flat, celery-like leaves on 24-inch-tall plants. This type is particularly favored for cooking. Parsley is a biennial hardy through Zone 6, but it is usually grown as an annual. Buy transplants or start parsley from seed, soaking the seed overnight in warm water before planting. Harvest individual stems as needed, picking the outermost ones.

Parsley.

- **Rosemary** (*Rosmarinus officinalis*) Rosemary is a woody, evergreen shrub, either upright or cascading, hardy through Zone 8. 'Arp', 'Salem' and 'Hill's Hardy' survive winter through Zone 6. Grow plants in pots and bring indoors in winter. Rosemary can grow 3 to 6 feet tall, with narrow gray-green and small blue or pink flowers. Grow rosemary from transplants or rooted cuttings.

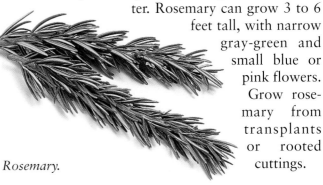

Rosemary.

- **Sage** (*Salvia officinalis*) Sage has a much more mellow, pleasant flavor when used fresh rather than dried. Sage is a woody perennial hardy through Zone 5. It grows to 24 inches tall. Beautiful stalks of edible purple flowers are borne in late spring. The pebbly, gray-green leaves are evergreen in mild winters. There are also varieties with purple or variegated leaves. Grow sage from transplants. Propagate new plants from old by rooting cuttings.

Sage.

- **Thyme** (*Thymus* spp. and cultivars) Thyme is a versatile perennial, hardy through Zone 5. Start with a rooted cutting or a pot-grown plant of a good culinary cultivar such as 'French' and 'English' or perhaps lemon, caraway and orange balsam. Thyme hugs the ground and grows only 12 inches tall. It also produces tiny pink, lavender or white flowers in midsummer that are edible.

Thyme.

CONTAINERS AND WINDOW BOXES

Growing pretty flowers in containers is low-labor fun. Heavy digging and weeding are not required and you can move your flowers around at will. In addition, container gardening demands little space, so it's the perfect way to let your gardening spirit soar in a small yard or patio setting.

Starting a Container Garden

Kick off the container gardening season in spring, when bedding plants are widely available. Choose containers that are as large as you can comfortably handle—large containers need less frequent watering than small ones. If weight is a worry, go with featherweight plastic containers. Many are available in earthy colors that mimic the appearance of heavier clay or stone.

Also buy plenty of bagged potting soil. These products contain little (if any) actual soil, so they do not pack down the way real soil does. Purchased potting soils usually are made of pulverized peat moss, composted organic matter, a little sand and perhaps some absorbent perlite or vermiculite. The result is a soft, moisture-retentive medium for pot-grown plants. If you're new to container gardening, try two or three different brands of potting soil until you find a favorite.

Pots of impatiens and begonia provide quiet beauty for a shady deck.

Garden Tip
Try Something New

Fan flower, properly known as *Scaevola*, stays covered with elegant blue flowers all summer, and actually grows better in pots than it does in the ground. Look for container-grown plants in nurseries in spring. Grow them in partial to full sun.

Scaevola 'Blue Wonder'.

1

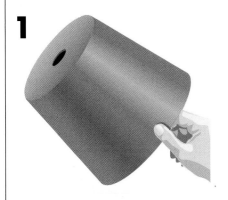

1 Choose a container with at least one drainage hole in the bottom through which excess water can escape.

2

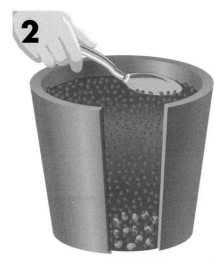

3

2 Fill the bottom half of the container with potting soil. Mix in some loose stones or broken pottery to give the container extra weight and improve drainage. Dampen thoroughly. Add potting soil to within ½ inch of the top. Tamp the pot to help settle the soil into the container.

3 Before planting container-grown plants, break apart the bottom half of the root ball and gently spread out the loose roots.

4

4 Your composition will be more lush and colorful if you crowd plants so that the root balls are only 2 inches apart. Make sure the highest roots are covered with at least ½ inch of potting soil.

5

5 Water the planted container thoroughly and allow the excess water to drain away. Drench the pot again after 20 minutes. Place the container in a dish filled with stones or gravel, or set it up on flat stones or bricks. Check to make sure the drainage holes are not blocked.

Water and Fertilizer

Because their root area is restricted, plants grown in containers need frequent watering and feeding. Each time you water, nutrients in the potting soil leach away. Replace these nutrients by using fertilizer spikes or pellets in the containers. Or mix a small amount of a time-release fertilizer into the potting soil before you fill your containers with plants. You can also simply mix a soluble fertilizer with the water you use for your plants. Add a half-ration of fertilizer to the water each time you moisten the soil in your pots.

Many gardeners alternate synthetic soluble fertilizer with an organic fertilizer such as fish emulsion. Every few weeks, you may want to treat your plants to a compost "tea tonic" (made by mixing a gallon of compost with 5 gallons water). This solution supplements other fertilizers, providing micronutrients and enzymes.

As plants grow larger and their roots fill the container, water may run out through the sides of the container before the roots receive adequate moisture. The best way to tell if this is happening is to lift the pot to see if it feels heavy. If a container still feels light after watering, soak it several times or place it in a tub filled with a few inches of water until the thirsty plants drink their fill.

Layered into a window box, yucca, geranium and trailing stems of vinca make great companions.

Mixing and Matching

It's fun to plant different annuals together in the same container. When creating a container bouquet, place upright plants, such as a geranium, near the center and flank with plants that grow into soft mounds, such as petunias. Finally, add small trailing plants such as lobelia or sweet alyssum at the pot's edge.

Try These

Amazing Annuals for Containers

Full Sun
Geranium
Petunia
Portulaca
Sweet alyssum
Verbena

Pink zonal geraniums.

Partial Sun
Begonia
Dusty miller
Lobelia
Pansy
Salvia

'Fluffy Ruffles' petunia.

Shade
Coleus
Impatiens
Nicotiana
Polka dot plant
Torenia

'Starbright' impatiens.

FRAGRANCE IN CONTAINERS

Gardening in containers is easy, and allows you to bring fragrance up close, whether in window boxes, hanging baskets, pots on the front porch or large planters on your deck or patio. The special group of plants that provide strong fragrance and grow well in containers includes annuals, perennials and a few shrubs and bulbs. Here we will provide a sufficient sample so that you can fill your containers with unfussy fragrant plants. Then sit back and reap compliments on your gardening flair and expertise.

Scented Geraniums

Scented geraniums (*Pelargonium* spp.) are grown for their leaves rather than their flowers. They are best handled as pot-grown perennials left outdoors in summer and kept indoors when temperatures drop below freezing.

Scented geranium leaves offer an amazing array of fragrances as well as shapes and textures, with over 200 species and cultivars. Many gardeners enjoy collecting these undemanding plants with fragrances that include rose, mint, lemon and even chocolate.

Scented geraniums do best in pots placed in full sun in spring and 50 percent shade in summer. Water them when the top ½ inch of soil is dry. Feed monthly from spring to autumn. Trim them to maintain the shape and size you want. For additional plants, take root cuttings. Winter plants indoors in bright light with nighttime temperatures of 60°F.

A trio of scented geraniums.

Gardenias

The gardenia is one of the most fragrant plants on earth. It is a tropical shrub that serves well as a summer patio plant, but it needs a cool indoor place to spend the winter. Most cultivars are hardy only to about 20°F. The cultivar commonly known as 'Radicans' (*G. jasminoides radicans*) is ideal for pots filled with potting soil amended with acidic peat moss. The best flowering period is early summer. Salt buildup in pots can be a problem; it is best cured by flushing out the containers with large amounts of water at least twice each summer. Water lightly during winter when the plants are indoors.

Gardenia blossoms.

Forced Bulbs

Plant fragrant hyacinths and paperwhite narcissus in pots in the fall. Dampen well, then place the pots in a cold place for at least six weeks. An unheated garage or trench dug in the ground, or a protected spot next to the side of your house, are good places for bulbs to spend a few cold weeks growing roots. Move the pots indoors in late winter, and treat them as sun-loving houseplants until they flower. Tazetta daffodils need little (if any) cold treatment, but the hyacinths and fragrant daffodils like 'Geranium' and 'Grand Soleil d'Or' must have at least six weeks of cold.

Fragrant hyacinths are naturals for small pots.

Fragrant purple heliotrope seems to burst from a nest of rosemary.

Fragrant Flowers for Container Bouquets

It's fun to combine fast-growing annual flowers in 15- to 24-inch pots, creating fragrant container bouquets. In devising your combinations, take into consideration color compatibility, growth habit and requirements, the time of day that you want scent and whether the scents might compete with each other.

Put taller plants toward the center of a large planter, or place a stake in the middle for plants that will grow more than 15 inches tall. Surround them with lower-growing plants, plus trailing plants toward the edges. For that luxurious look, include more plants in a container than you would in a similar space directly in the garden. The following selections are widely available and easy to grow.

- **Flowering tobacco** (*Nicotiana* spp. and cultivars) From the rosettes of oval leaves rise stalks with trumpet-shaped, 1- to 3-inch flowers emitting an exotic fragrance at night. Flowers close during the day. For containers, look for 2- to 3-foot-tall *N. alata*, which is not as tall and lanky as the other fragrant species. You may need to start it

from seed. Many dwarf bedding-type varieties are not fragrant.

- **Stock** (*Matthiola incana*) This old-fashioned flower produces intensely sweet, clove-scented flowers. Stocks need cool weather; they melt away in high heat. The 15- to 30-inch-tall plants benefit from staking or other support, such as a small wire cage placed inside the container.

Nicotiana.

Sweet alyssum.

- **Sweet alyssum** (*Lobularia maritima*) A rich honey scent floats like a cloud above rounded clusters of tiny white, pink, magenta or purple flowers on sprawling, low-growing stems. Add this versatile plant to almost any container as a cascading edging plant. Alyssum grows 2 to 12 inches tall and 8 to 12 inches wide.

- **Heliotrope** (*Heliotropium arborescens*) Hundreds of tiny, vanilla-scented, purple flowers form clusters to 4 inches across. The woody, openly-branched plants grow to 18 inches tall and 12 inches wide. Actually a tropical perennial, this flower is usually sold among bedding plants in spring.

- **Pinks** (*Dianthus* spp. including *D. plumaris* and *D. superbus*) These short-lived perennials produce a spicy carnation-like scent when they bloom in spring. They are easy to grow in large containers filled with a sandy mix amended with lime. They grow 1 to 2 feet tall.

Garden pinks.

- **Petunia** (*Petunia* hybrids) This popular annual often has a strong vanilla scent in the evening, especially white, violet-blue and purple varieties. Both bush and trailing types are available. Fragrance varies among varieties and colors: Be prepared for surprises. A few fragrant selections include 'Primetime Purple', 'White Cascade' and 'Pink Wave'.

Heliotrope takes center stage.

Petunias.

MAXIMIZING FRAGRANCE

To make the most of fragrant flowers and leaves in the garden, the air must be fairly still.

Slight breezes may gently bring the scents to you, but strong winds quickly disperse them.

To shelter a garden area, consider installing a fence or establishing a windbreak of evergreen

or deciduous trees or shrubs. Some of these may be specially selected for their fragrance.

Tarragon's savory flavor is matched by its fresh herbal fragrance.

Fencing in Fragrance

If you don't have the space for a windbreak, consider building a small south-facing length of wall or fence, which will reflect and radiate heat. In cooler regions such as the Pacific Northwest or New England, many gardeners find that a windbreak surrounding a wall shelters the garden from wind, while the wall is effective in warming the garden. This extra warmth heightens the fragrance of many favorite flowers.

Adding a paved surface helps as well. Include a bench or seat in this area so that you can linger, breathing in the delicious fragrances.

Location and Height

"The closer the better" is the motto of growing fragrant plants in the garden. Place them near the deck or patio, beside the front and back doors, and in window boxes. Make sure some of your favorite scented plants are near benches in the garden, the porch swing and around any outdoor dining area.

Furnish outdoor living areas with fragrant plants so that they are always close enough to enjoy at nose level.

Thyme is a tough little herb suitable for growing in crevices among steppingstones.

Simple Touches

This aspect of touch provides several landscaping opportunities. Plant creeping herbs, like different species of thyme or chamomile, among stepping-stones or under and around a garden seat. Let larger plants like lavender, mint or rosemary spill over a garden path, so that the foliage is easily brushed as you walk along.

Containers of Scent

For plantings farther from the house, choose a site in the garden where you'll frequently go. Whenever possible, plant low-growing plants in raised beds or planters so they are a little closer to nose height. Pots of fragrant plants bring mobility to fragrance, plus it's easy to put them on raised surfaces such as the tops of low tables or walls.

The foliage of many plants also brings scent to the garden. The main difference between foliage and flowers is that foliage usually must be touched to release the scent. The main exceptions are the herb garden or an evergreen planting on a hot, still summer day.

Scented geraniums are well suited to containers, so you can amass a large collection in a small amount of space.

Beneath this pergola, there is no question that one should stop to smell the roses—and the wisteria too.

Surround Yourself with Scent

Arbors, pergolas, arches and tunnels are another way to surround yourself with fragrance. What pleasure to walk or sit under wisteria, honeysuckle, climbing roses or arched laburnum trees. And don't overlook the possibilities of picket fences, trellises or low walls with planting pockets for bringing fragrance closer.

Night and Day

When considering which fragrant plants to grow, keep the time of best scent in mind. A garden overflowing with fragrance might never be appreciated if the gardener leaves the house early in the morning to go to work. For this person, it would be advantageous to plant those flowers that exude their scent during the evening hours. Some evening favorites include flowering tobacco, four o'clocks, evening primrose and dame's rocket. Some plants that you might think are not fragrant, like common garden phlox and some daylilies, become well scented at night.

Conversely, the gardener who is out at dawn wandering among the plants should concentrate on day-scented flowers, which include most of the fragrant plants other than the night-scented varieties.

Lightly fragrant four o'clocks show their festive colors from late afternoon until the following day when the sun shines brightly.

The Language of Fragrance

Through the centuries, people have attempted to create standard categories of fragrances in order to better describe them and remove at least some subjectivity. With these categories, you'll be better able to differentiate floral scents from one another.

- **Balsamic** - Found in leaves that contain menthol or minty essential oils: mints, lavender, sages, rosemary, wormwood, balsam and eucalyptus.

- **Fruited** - Found in flowers or leaves of a wide range of plants: grape hyacinth, magnolia, flowering fruits, sweet olive and fruit-scented geraniums.

Tansy, chives, lemon balm, tarragon and sage create a mix of fragrances in this herb border.

Scented geraniums release soft fragrance when the leaves are touched.

- **Heavy** - Found in flowers with strong, penetrating perfume: gardenia, orange blossom, jasmine and tuberose.

- **Honeyed** - Found in many different flowers: hawthorn, barberry, Oregon grape holly and hybrid musk roses.

- **Rose** - The scent that predominates in a few old European garden roses and a few other plants: some peonies, winter honeysuckle and leather-leaf mahonia.

- **Spicy** - Found in leaves and flowers, often combined with other scents: carnations, pinks, azaleas, fennel and nasturtium.

- **Sweet** - Found in flowers, grasses and ferns: fringe tree, elder, honeysuckle, heliotrope and crinum.

- **Unique** - Similar to heavy scents (described above), but even more distinct and refined: lily-of-the-valley, sweet pea, some iris, wisteria and common lilac.

- **Violet** - Found in the flowers or roots of only a few plants: sweet violet, Siberian crabapple and orris root.

Try These
Woody Plants for Summer Fragrance

- **Magnolia** (*Magnolia virginiana*), spring to late summer. Zones 5 to 9. This native magnolia tree seldom grows taller than 30 feet. Dwarf cultivars are available. It is deciduous in the North and evergreen in the South. Commonly known as sweet bay magnolia, it bears lemon-scented flowers sporadically all summer. Thrives in wet soils and low spots.

Sweet bay magnolia.

- **Summersweet** (*Clethra alnifolia*), summer. Zones 3 to 9. This native shrub or small tree is perfect for wet, shady areas. White or pink panicles of flowers develop dependably in midsummer and are attractive to butterflies. Be patient, for this plant is a slow grower.

- **Butterfly bush** (*Buddleia* spp. and cultivars), summer to autumn. Zones 5 to 9. Long spikes of yellow, lavender, purple or white flowers with pungent fragrance appear on new wood and attract butterflies and hummingbirds. Prune back hard in winter. Will grow in any sunny, well-drained location.

Butterfly bush.

SUMMER COLOR COMBOS

If you don't want to guess about color, try these tried-and-true plant combinations.

Red and White

Crisp and neat, red and white always looks clean and manicured, but carries plenty of energy too. Frame a small drift of red geraniums with white petunias, or make the most of partial shade by flanking red salvias with white impatiens.

Clean contrast—between white and deep, saturated colors such as magenta (shown), deep pink and red— gives a flower bed a crisp, tailored appearance.

Red and white always work well together. A few pink begonias share the spotlight with more high-contrast colors.

Red and Blue

Red zinnias may look a little coarse on their own, but not in the company of blue salvia. Ageratum, a common summer bedding plant, is a dependable source of blue for combining with red geraniums. Pair blue pansies with any shade of red for beautiful special effects.

Yellow and Blue

Yellow daffodils and blue pansies are a classic rendition of this combination. In summer beds, edge yellow melampodium with blue ageratum, or use blue sage with yellow zinnias or sunflowers.

Pink and Gray

Pink is never wishy-washy in the company of gray foliage plants such as dusty miller and stachys. Full, bold pinks work best, but gray can bring out the best in baby pink impatiens too, especially in partial shade where natural darkness provides needed contrast.

Pink petunias glow in the company of soft gray foliage plants such as dusty miller or artemisia.

Orange and Purple

Orange is never a problem color when paired with deep purple. In hot summer areas particularly, pair orange zinnias or sulphur cosmos with purple angelonia or Mexican bush sage. In spring, orange tulips look great in the company of blue pansies.

Garden Tip
Color Wheel

Opposites attract. That's the idea behind the color wheel, a handy way to know if colors will match, give good contrast or clash. Colors directly opposite each other on the color wheel are high contrast, or complementary, colors. If you place a triangle in the center of the wheel and rotate it around, colors at each point of the triangle are a safe three-way combination. It's important to pay attention to subtle differences in hues too. So use the color wheel as a general guide, but let your eyes make the final decision when you choose plants.

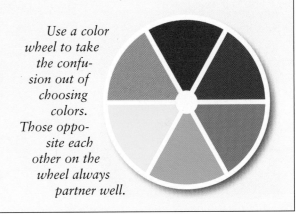

Use a color wheel to take the confusion out of choosing colors. Those opposite each other on the wheel always partner well.

BUILD AN EASY WATER GARDEN

Water gardens are popular, and with good reason. Even a small water garden becomes an irresistible focal point in the landscape. You can stock a water garden with flowering plants, foliage plants and a few little fish to control mosquitoes. Regardless of what you may have heard about pumps, filters and other electric gear, anyone can create natural ponds that require no cords, and no upkeep beyond occasional cleaning.

Building a Water Garden

The first thing you need is a way to contain water. Rigid plastic forms are tempting, but they must be installed in a hole with a level bottom that fits them like a glove. Flexible rubber liners are much easier to handle, and can be used to make either a pond set down in the ground or an above-ground pond like the one described on pages 140-141.

Digging an in-ground pond is simple, though you may be surprised at how long it takes to dig a large hole with a level top edge.

To build an above-ground water garden using landscape timbers, digging is limited to leveling the soil upon which the frame will rest, and perhaps excavating a few inches of soil if you want or need a very deep pond. Where winters are cold or

Flexible plastic liners makes it simple for anyone to build a water garden or fish pond to suit any site.

Even a simple plastic-formed pool can transform your garden's ambiance with the sound of water.

summers are very hot, make at least part of your water garden at least 16 inches deep. At this depth, the water at the very bottom of the pond will not freeze solid in winter (in most climates) nor become too warm in summer, so fish and hardy plants stand a good chance of surviving both types of weather extremes.

Bringing in Fish

Hardy little goldfish, called comets, are the easiest fish to keep in a small water garden. If you buy them at a pet shop in early summer and release them into settled water, expect about a 60 percent survival rate. Goldfish that survive their first week outdoors are likely to live for several years as long as the water at the bottom of the pond does not freeze hard in the winter. Be careful not to overstock your pond or to overfeed your fish. The 4-by 8-foot pond shown on page 140 can comfortably support 3 to 6 goldfish (depending on their size), which can be fed once a day in warm weather. In cold weather, they will get sufficient nutrients from plants and water. Goldfish often reproduce in outdoor ponds that include plenty of submerged plants.

Koi are a more active species and need more room than comets. Use koi only in large ponds where they have plenty of room to swim. Koi need pond water at least two feet deep, with a surface area greater than 24 square feet.

Comet goldfish.

Building a Water Garden

This project requires only a few hours of work, though you may want to complete it in stages. The structure is really quite easy to build in that it is not complex at all. However, you will need a strong back and strong set of hands for the initial stages; feel free to "borrow" some from a friend or relative!

1-2

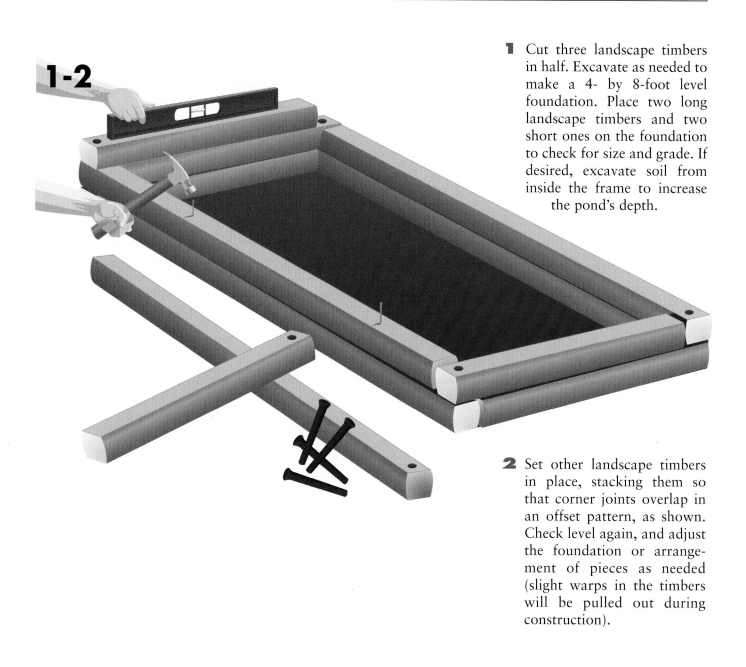

1 Cut three landscape timbers in half. Excavate as needed to make a 4- by 8-foot level foundation. Place two long landscape timbers and two short ones on the foundation to check for size and grade. If desired, excavate soil from inside the frame to increase the pond's depth.

2 Set other landscape timbers in place, stacking them so that corner joints overlap in an offset pattern, as shown. Check level again, and adjust the foundation or arrangement of pieces as needed (slight warps in the timbers will be pulled out during construction).

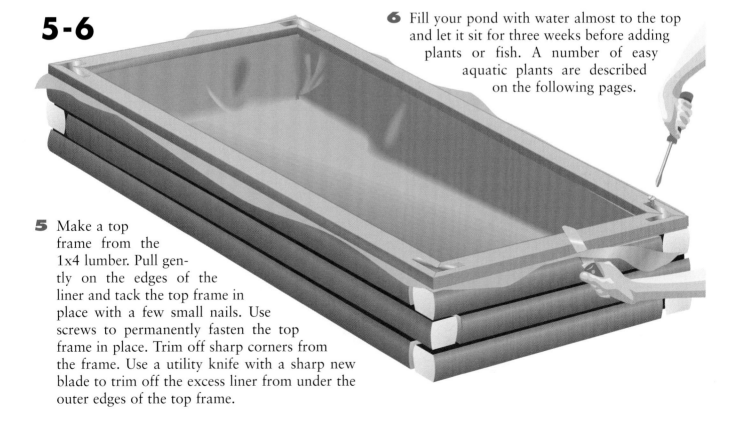

3-4

3 Drill ½-inch holes through each corner, and pound in rebar stakes until they protrude only 6 inches from the top. Remove the top tier of timbers. Drill guide holes for two nails in the second-tier timbers on each side, and nail the second tier to the foundation level. Put the top tier of timbers back in place, and nail them to the second tier. Pound in rebar stakes until they are even with the top.

4 Spread liner in the pond, folding corners as needed to make them as flat as possible. Slowly fill the pond with water to within 8 inches of the top, allowing the weight of the water to stretch the liner as the pond fills. Do not trim the excess from the edges of the liner yet.

5-6

5 Make a top frame from the 1x4 lumber. Pull gently on the edges of the liner and tack the top frame in place with a few small nails. Use screws to permanently fasten the top frame in place. Trim off sharp corners from the frame. Use a utility knife with a sharp new blade to trim off the excess liner from under the outer edges of the top frame.

6 Fill your pond with water almost to the top and let it sit for three weeks before adding plants or fish. A number of easy aquatic plants are described on the following pages.

PLANTS FOR A NATURAL POND

Algae are tiny plants that give pond water a green, cloudy appearance. If you want a healthy natural pond in which one life form helps another by providing food or habitat, a bit of algae is a good thing. But too much algae ruins a pond's mirror effect, and makes the water so murky that you cannot see your fish. As your pond develops into a unique ecosystem, plant foliage on the pond's surface will block light to the water, which will in turn limit the proliferation of algae. Excessive algae is naturally discouraged if at least 60 percent of the water's surface is covered with plants.

All the aquatic plants that produce colorful blooms grow best in full sun, or in a half day of sun in very warm climates. Numerous native plants will grow in partial shade, especially along the shallow edges or in containers set on bricks to raise them to just under the water's surface.

Types of Aquatic Plants

Plants that grow in water are classified into the four groups listed here. Using different types of plants will help keep your water garden biologically balanced, and makes it look great too. Most hardy aquatic plants become dormant in winter and re-emerge in spring. In very cold climates, you may need to drain your water garden in fall and restock it with new plants and fish in late spring.

ROOTED
FLOATERS

EMERGENT

SUBMERGED
PLANTS

FREE FLOATERS

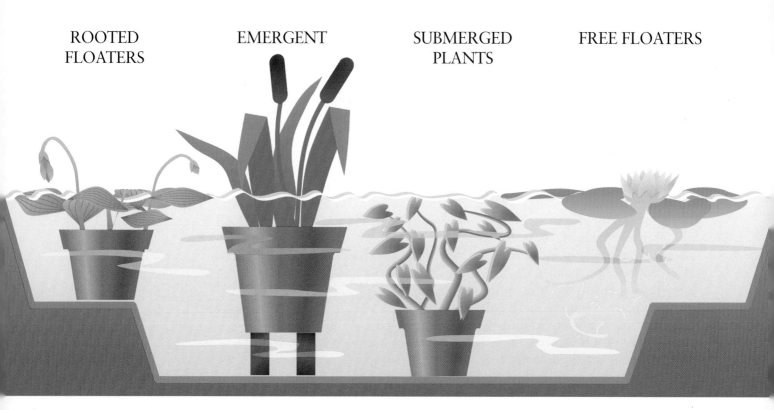

Emergent Plants

This class includes most upright plants found in boggy places, such as cattails and water iris. Their roots are constantly under water, but their leaves and stems grow above the surface. Grow emergent plants in pots set below the surface. Place them to provide vertical interest in your water garden. These species are dependable and hardy, and there are a number of native species.

- **Iris** (*Iris* species) Flat upright leaves are topped with elegant flowers in spring which may be blue, purple, white or yellow. Some species and hybrids are hardy to Zone 4. All grow best with their roots covered with 2 to 4 inches of water.

- **Dwarf cattail** (*Typha minima*) Thin grassy leaves stand straight up, and usually produce velvety brown cattails (or catkins) in summer. Cold winters increase catkin production. Dwarf cattail grows best in 12 to 14 inches of water, and plants are hardy to Zone 3. Divide clumps in spring, planting them to individual submerged containers.

- **Arrowheads** (*Sagittaria* spp.) Sometimes called water plantain, arrowheads have fibrous roots, leaves shaped like arrowheads and flowers that develop on upright spikes. Several native species are hardy to Zone 4, and typically produce white flowers in summer. Persistent but not aggressive, arrowheads are ideal for shallow edges.

Dwarf cattail.

Water iris.

Arrowhead.

Rooted Floaters

These plants have roots anchored in mucky soil, but their leaves float at or slightly above the surface. Popular blooming plants including water lilies and lotus fit into this group. Grow them in broad pots filled halfway with clay and humus in 10 to 18 inches of water.

- **Dwarf lotus** (*Nelumbo* spp. and cultivars) Flat green leaves rise above the water's surface on stout stems, and produce exotic blooms in summer after warm weather has prevailed for several weeks. Dwarf forms are mostly native to China, and will survive winter at the bottom of ponds that do not freeze solid. Plant dormant roots in containers in spring.

Dwarf lotus.

- **Dwarf water lilies** (*Nymphaea* spp. and cultivars) Flat leaves with single notches float at the surface. Showy flowers appear in summer, and many selections repeat bloom. Dwarf cultivars grow well in water only a few inches deeper than their containers. Hardy to Zone 3, provided the water does not freeze solid.

Dwarf water lily.

Free Floaters

No pots are needed to grow these plants, which form colonies that station themselves at the surface. Roots filter nutrients available in the water. These plants are often very vigorous and spread rapidly.

- **Floating heart** (*Nymphoides peltata*) Small yellow flowers rise above heart-shaped green leaves. As roots find muddy earth on the bottom of the pond, colonies become large and vigorous. Hardy to Zone 6.

- **Water clover** (*Marsilea mutica*) Thrives in partial shade where other water plants struggle. Pretty four-leafed clovers float at the surface. This plant is not reliably winter hardy in cold climates, but grows vigorously from spring to fall.

Water clover.

Parrot's feather.

Submerged Plants

Most plant parts remain below water because the limp stems require water for support. Roots often anchor themselves in pebbles or silt, but the plants can grow with free-floating roots. Submerged plants work as natural water filters, taking up excess nutrients directly from the water, and make excellent cover for breeding fish.

- **Elodea** (*Elodea canadensis*) Very hardy, sometimes invasive, but a real asset to ponds that tend to go green with algae. Also a fine host plant for breeding fish. Native to North America. Prune or thin out excess plants in fall and early summer.

- **Parrot's feather** (*Myriophyllum aquatica*) Ferny blue-green foliage rises a few inches above the surface, while roots and submerged stems spread through the water. Tolerates partial shade. Hardy to Zone 6.

SUMMER

ENTERTAINING

Summer was made for entertaining. Maybe it's a couple friends on the deck or patio. Maybe it's a big, fun group for a Fourth of July celebration. Either way, you want to be able to make great food and wow your guests, but still have time and energy to enjoy the event and the weather. That's what these incredibly quick, easy and delicious menus are all about. Make-ahead ideas and tips are included, to save you even more time and work.

Facing page: Mediterranean Bread Salad and Pesto Grilled Shrimp Kabobs, part of the Grilling Magic and S'More menu, page 164

A Star-Spangled Event

Fireworks light up the sky and this menu sparkles on the 4th of July! These recipes make a summer celebration that is both colorful and delicious.

Menu

~ Herb Marinated Chicken Breasts
~ Red, White and Blue Salsa
~ Parmesan Rosemary Focaccia
~ Tropical Fruit Foster
~ Starry Grilled Pound Cake

Entertains 8

HERB MARINATED CHICKEN BREASTS

Chicken absorbs the marinade's flavor quickly. Since chicken is naturally tender, be careful not to marinate it too long or it will turn mushy.

8   boneless skinless chicken breasts
¼   cup extra-virgin olive oil
1   tablespoon white wine
1   tablespoon lemon juice
1   tablespoon Dijon mustard
½   teaspoon dried thyme

1 Place chicken breasts in large resealable plastic bag.

2 In small bowl, combine oil, wine, lemon juice, mustard and thyme; mix well. Pour mixture over chicken; seal bag. Refrigerate 15 minutes.

3 Heat grill. Remove chicken from marinade; discard marinade. Place chicken on grill 4 to 6 inches from medium coals or on gas grill over medium heat. Grill, turning once, 10 minutes or until internal temperature reaches 160°F.

Serves 8.
Preparation time: 10 minutes.
Ready to serve: 35 minutes.
Per serving: 155 calories, 5 g total fat (1 g saturated fat), 65 mg cholesterol, 65 mg sodium, 0 g fiber.

Menu Tip
• Marinating meats is super easy when you use a sturdy, zippered plastic bag. For the *Herb Marinated Chicken Breasts*, place chicken and marinade in the bag, then press out as much air as possible. This pulls the liquid around meat so the marinating process is more effective, and it also makes the bag easier to store in the refrigerator.

Before the Event
Prepare the marinade earlier in the day and store in the refrigerator until you're ready to add the chicken.

RED, WHITE AND BLUE SALSA

This is the perfect salsa for a patriotic holiday, but it tastes so delicious you'll be serving

it at other times of the year too.

¼ cup sherry vinegar
¼ cup extra-virgin olive oil
¼ cup packed brown sugar
2 cups sliced fresh strawberries
2 cups blueberries
½ cup minced red onion
½ cup chopped toasted pecans

1 In medium bowl, whisk vinegar, oil and brown sugar. Add strawberries, blueberries, red onion and pecans; toss to combine. Serve mixture over chicken.

Serves 8.
Preparation time: 15 minutes.
Ready to serve: 15 minutes.
Per serving: 170 calories, 12 g total fat (1.5 g saturated fat), 0 mg cholesterol, 5 mg sodium, 2.5 g fiber.

Menu Tip
- To toast pecans, spread on baking sheet; bake at 375°F 5 minutes or until lightly browned. Cool.

Before the Event
Make *Red, White and Blue Salsa* the morning of the party.

PARMESAN ROSEMARY FOCACCIA

Focaccia is an herbed, cheese-topped Italian bread. Frozen bread dough makes great focaccia if you accent it with just a few additional ingredients.

1 tablespoon extra-virgin olive oil, plus more for drizzling
2 teaspoons cornmeal
1 (1-lb.) loaf frozen bread dough, thawed
2 tablespoons freshly grated Parmesan cheese
1 tablespoon fresh rosemary or 1 teaspoon dried
⅛ teaspoon kosher (coarse) salt

1 Heat oven to 375°F.

2 Brush baking sheet with 1 tablespoon of the oil; sprinkle with cornmeal.

3 Pat dough into 10-inch circle; place on baking sheet. Drizzle dough with additional olive oil; sprinkle with Parmesan, rosemary and salt. Let rise 30 minutes.

4 Press all over dough with fingers. Bake 20 minutes or until golden.

Serves 8.
Preparation time: 10 minutes.
Ready to serve: 60 minutes.
Per serving: 175 calories, 4.5 g total fat (1 g saturated fat), 2 mg cholesterol, 360 mg sodium, 1.5 g fiber.

Before the Event

Make *Parmesan Rosemary Focaccia* a day ahead.

TROPICAL FRUIT FOSTER

Tropical fruits, such as mangoes, were once as rare as palm trees in Alaska. Now they are available in most supermarket produce departments. But don't worry if you can't get mangoes — just add more pineapple and bananas to the sauce. Or be adventurous and try different fruits that you like.

½	cup (1 stick) butter
1	cup packed dark brown sugar
½	cup orange juice
2	cups diced fresh pineapple
2	cups diced mango
4	bananas, sliced
2	quarts vanilla ice cream

1 In large skillet, melt butter over medium-high heat. Add brown sugar, orange juice, pineapple, mango and bananas; sauté 3 minutes or until just heated through. Serve warm over ice cream.

Serves 8.
Preparation time: 13 minutes.
Ready to serve: 15 minutes.
Per serving: 575 calories, 26.5 g total fat (16 g saturated fat), 90 mg cholesterol, 195 mg sodium, 2.5 g fiber.

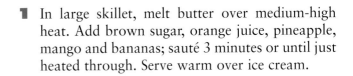

Before the Event

Peel and cube the pineapple and mango the day before, then cover and refrigerate.

STARRY GRILLED POUND CAKE

A star cookie cutter turns a great pound cake into a sparkling dessert.

1   (1-lb.) pound cake
½   cup (1 stick) butter, melted
1   teaspoon ground ginger

1 With serrated bread knife, cut pound cake into horizontal slices, about 1 inch thick. Using 2½-inch cookie cutter, cut out 8 stars.

2 In small bowl, combine butter and ginger. Using pastry brush, coat pound cake "stars" with butter mixture.

3 Place pound cake "stars" on medium-hot grill about 30 seconds per side or until golden. Serve with *Tropical Fruit Foster* (page 153) and ice cream.

Serves 8.
Preparation time: 10 minutes.
Ready to serve: 15 minutes.
Per serving: 575 calories, 26.5 g total fat (16 g saturated fat), 90 mg cholesterol, 195 mg sodium, 2.5 g fiber.

Before the Event

Cut *Starry Grilled Pound Cake*, then cover it until it's ready to grill.

STRAIGHT FROM THE FARMERS' MARKET

A trip to the farmers' market is a summer treat in itself. And here's a very special way to enjoy summer's best vegetables and fruits, right on your own table.

Menu

~ Mushroom Bruschetta
~ Fresh Corn Pasta
~ Summer Corn Relish
~ Pan-Seared Scallops
~ Double Blueberry Tart

Entertains 8

MUSHROOM BRUSCHETTA

Wild mushrooms offer distinct flavor, but are quite expensive. Mix them with less expensive white mushrooms to enhance flavor without busting your budget.

¼ cup extra-virgin olive oil
2 shallots, minced
2 garlic cloves, minced
3 tablespoons finely chopped fresh tarragon
1 lb. mixed fresh domestic and wild
    mushrooms, chopped
16 slices French bread, about ¼ inch thick

1 In large skillet, heat 2 tablespoons of the oil over medium-high heat until hot. Add shallots, garlic and tarragon; sauté 1 minute. Stir in mushrooms. Cook, stirring occasionally, about 8 minutes or until shallots are brown.

2 Heat broiler.

3 Brush both sides of bread with remaining 2 tablespoons oil. Place bread under broiler about 2 minutes per side or until golden. Spoon shallot mixture evenly over toast; serve.

Serves 8.
Preparation time: 15 minutes.
Ready to serve: 29 minutes.
Per serving: 100 calories, 7.5 g total fat (1 g saturated fat), 0 mg cholesterol, 50 mg sodium, 1 g fiber.

Before the Event

Make mushrooms a day ahead and warm through before serving.

FRESH CORN PASTA

Taking corn off the cob is easy. Just cut off the wide end of the cob to make it flat, then stand it on that flat end and cut down the ear with a knife, slicing off the kernels.

1	(16-oz.) pkg. linguine
12	strips thick-sliced bacon, crisply cooked, chopped
4	cups fresh corn kernels
1	medium onion, chopped
1	garlic clove, chopped
½	cup reduced-sodium chicken broth
½	cup cream
1	cup Parmesan curls (optional)

1 In large pot of boiling water, cook linguine according to package directions; drain.

2 Meanwhile, in large skillet, heat bacon, corn, onion and garlic over medium-high heat; cook about 5 minutes or until vegetables are tender.

3 Add chicken broth and cream to skillet; cook about 2 minutes or until sauce thickens. Add linguine; toss to combine. Arrange on serving platter; garnish with Parmesan curls, if desired.

Serves 8.
Preparation time: 15 minutes.
Ready to serve: 32 minutes.
Per serving: 450 calories, 15.5 g total fat (6.5 g saturated fat), 30 mg cholesterol, 570 mg sodium, 4 g fiber.

Before the Event

Cook the linguine a day ahead, rinse and refrigerate until you're ready to serve. Cook bacon ahead and refrigerate until you're ready to use it.

SUMMER CORN RELISH

The sweet corn season is so short, you should use every opportunity to enjoy this quintessential summer treat. Here's another chance to eat corn, now in a relish that complements this menu's pasta and scallops.

2   tablespoons extra-virgin olive oil
1   cup fresh corn kernels
1   green bell pepper, cored, chopped
2   tomatoes, seeded, chopped

1 In medium pan, heat oil over medium-high heat until hot. Add corn; cook about 4 minutes.

2 Add bell pepper; heat an additional minute.

3 Remove pan from heat; add tomato. Serve with *Pan-Seared Scallops* (below).

Serves 8.
Preparation time: 5 minutes.
Ready to serve: 10 minutes.
Per serving: 55 calories, 3.5 g total fat (0.5 g saturated fat), 0 mg cholesterol, 4 mg sodium, 1 g fiber.

Before the Event
Sauté the peppers and corn earlier in the day.

PAN-SEARED SCALLOPS

Sea scallops are large and remain tender when cooked. When buying scallops, look for a creamy white color and a sweet, fresh smell.

2   lb. sea scallops, muscle removed
2   tablespoons chopped fresh thyme
1   teaspoon salt
2   tablespoons extra-virgin olive oil

1 Dry scallops with paper towels.

2 In medium bowl, toss scallops with thyme and salt.

3 In large skillet, heat oil over medium-high heat until hot. Add scallops; sauté about 4 minutes or until golden brown.

Serves 8.
Preparation time: 6 minutes.
Ready to serve: 10 minutes.
Per serving: 110 calories, 4.5 g total fat (0.5 g saturated fat), 25 mg cholesterol, 480 mg sodium, 1 g fiber.

Before the Event
Cook the scallops earlier in the day. Refrigerate and serve chilled, or tossed with the warm pasta at the last minute.

DOUBLE BLUEBERRY TART

Do you like your blueberries tart and crunchy or sweet and saucy? Have them both ways in this tart!

Pastry Dough

1½   cups all-purpose flour
½   cup (1 stick) unsalted butter, cold and cut into slices
¼   teaspoon salt
⅓   cup very cold water

Filling

4   cups blueberries
2   tablespoons lemon juice
¾   cup sugar
3   tablespoons cornstarch
¼   teaspoon ground ginger

1 Heat oven to 400°F.

2 In bowl, mix flour, butter and salt very lightly with pastry blender, so that butter pieces remain visible throughout flour. Add cold water; mix very quickly until dough coheres. Form into round; wrap with plastic wrap. Refrigerate 30 minutes.

3 Roll out dough; press into bottom and up sides of 9-inch pie plate. Bake 10 minutes or until golden.

4 Meanwhile, in medium saucepan, combine 2 cups of the blueberries, lemon juice, sugar, cornstarch and ginger; cook over medium heat about 2 minutes or until berries pop and filling thickens.

5 Transfer mixture from pan to large bowl; let cool 5 minutes.

6 Place remaining 2 cups blueberries in pastry crust. Pour cooled filling over fresh berries to cover. Refrigerate 1 hour before serving.

Serves 8.
Preparation time: 20 minutes.
Ready to serve: 30 minutes.
Per serving: 310 calories, 12 g total fat (7.5 g saturated fat), 30 mg cholesterol, 80 mg sodium, 2.5 g fiber.

Menu Tip

- To ensure that the pastry shell in the *Double Blueberry Tart* does not get soggy, paint the inside bottom of the baked, cooled tart shell with about 2 tablespoons melted currant or apple jelly.

Before the Event

Prepare the tart the day before and store in the refrigerator. This will make it firm and easier to serve.

GRILLING MAGIC AND S'MORE

It's summertime, so get out the grill and invite some friends over to enjoy a menu that sails around the Mediterranean but ends up right back at home.

Menu

~ Endive with Red Pepper Hummus
~ Mediterranean Bread Salad
~ Pesto Grilled Shrimp Kabobs
~ Lemon Rice with Pine Nuts
~ Newfangled S'Mores

Entertains 6

ENDIVE WITH RED PEPPER HUMMUS

Tahini is sesame paste — think peanut butter made with ground sesame seeds. It is an essential ingredient in Middle Eastern cooking.

1	(15-oz.) can garbanzo beans, drained, rinsed
1	roasted red bell pepper
2	garlic cloves, peeled
¼	cup fresh lemon juice
¼	cup extra-virgin olive oil
2	tablespoons tahini
1	teaspoon salt
3 to 4	medium heads Belgian endive, root ends cut off, leaves separated

1 Place garbanzo beans, roasted pepper, garlic, lemon juice, oil, tahini and salt in blender; puree until smooth. Chill until ready to serve.

2 Serve surrounded by endive leaves for dipping.

Serves 6.
Preparation time: 10 minutes.
Ready to serve: 15 minutes.
Per serving: 225 calories, 13.5 g total fat (2 g saturated fat), 0 mg cholesterol, 550 mg sodium, 9 g fiber.

Menu Tip
- Substitute pita wedges for the endive leaves in *Endive with Red Pepper Hummus*.

Before the Event
Make the hummus a day ahead, cover and refrigerate.

MEDITERRANEAN BREAD SALAD

Traditional Italian bread salad takes on a decidedly Greek flavor when you add feta cheese and kalamata olives. Any rustic style bread would be fine with this menu, but this rustic olive bread adds an interesting and aesthetic element.

Salad
2   cups cubed (1 inch) rustic olive bread
6   cups assorted salad greens
1   yellow or orange bell pepper, diced
1   cucumber, peeled, seeded, diced
½   cup pitted kalamata olives
1   cup (4 oz.) crumbled feta cheese

Pesto
2   garlic cloves, chopped
1   cup fresh basil, chopped
¼   cup freshly grated Parmesan cheese
¼   cup extra-virgin olive oil
2   tablespoons pine nuts or walnuts
¼   teaspoon salt
¼   teaspoon freshly ground pepper
⅓   cup extra-virgin olive oil

1 In large bowl, toss bread, greens, bell pepper, cucumber, olives and feta.

2 Place garlic, basil, Parmesan cheese, oil, pine nuts, salt and pepper in blender, food processor or mini-chopper; process until ingredients are pureed.

3 In small bowl, combine pesto and oil; pour over salad and toss to combine.

Serves 6.
Preparation time: 20 minutes.
Ready to serve: 25 minutes.
Per serving: 255 calories, 22 g total fat (6.5 g saturated fat), 25 mg cholesterol, 470 mg sodium, 2 g fiber.

Before the Event

Prepare the salad ingredients early in the day, then toss together and add dressing when you're ready to serve it.

PESTO GRILLED SHRIMP KABOBS

Fresh basil, garlic, pine nuts, olive oil and Parmesan cheese comprise pesto. The sauce is available in most grocery stores in the refrigerated section. It gives a great deal of flavor with very little effort.

2   lb. shelled, deveined uncooked large shrimp
⅓   cup prepared *Pesto* (page 167)

1 Heat grill.

2 In large bowl, toss shrimp with pesto to coat.

3 Place shrimp on water-soaked bamboo skewers. Place shrimp on gas grill over medium heat or on charcoal grill 4 to 6 inches from medium coals. Cook, turning once, 3 to 4 minutes or until shrimp turns pink.

Serves 6.
Preparation time: 10 minutes.
Ready to serve: 17 minutes.
Per serving: 190 calories, 9.5 g total fat (2 g saturated fat), 220 mg cholesterol, 295 mg sodium, 0 g fiber.

Menu Tip
- Bamboo skewers are inexpensive, and perfect for grilling. Soak them in water for about 30 minutes so they do not burn on the grill.

Before the Event
Clean shrimp and marinate them in pesto the night before.

LEMON RICE WITH PINE NUTS

This rice, with its refreshing and lemony taste, is very versatile. Serve it hot, but it tastes equally good cold. You choose!

2   cups long-grain rice
1   tablespoon grated lemon peel
2   tablespoons lemon juice
1   tablespoon extra-virgin olive oil
½   cup minced green onions
¼   cup toasted pine nuts
⅛   teaspoon salt
⅛   teaspoon freshly ground pepper

1 Cook rice according to package directions.

2 Meanwhile, combine lemon peel, lemon juice, oil, green onions and pine nuts in large bowl.

3 Fluff cooked rice with fork; add to large bowl. Toss to combine. Season with salt and pepper.

Serves 6.
Preparation time: 10 minutes.
Ready to serve: 30 minutes.
Per serving: 300 calories, 6 g total fat (1 g saturated fat), 0 mg cholesterol, 775 mg sodium, 1.5 g fiber.

Menu Tip
- Toast pine nuts in batches in dry skillet. Or place pine nuts in 15x10x1-inch pan; bake at 350°F 5 minutes or until golden brown, stirring occasionally.

Before the Event
Prepare *Lemon Rice with Pine Nuts* earlier in the day, then warm the dish in the oven just before serving.

NEWFANGLED S'MORES

Let the child in you revisit an old campfire favorite. These s'mores have been updated with some new ingredients. But the gooiest, most important element — hot toasted marshmallows — remains unchanged.

3   (3-oz.) white chocolate bars, halved
12   squares chocolate graham crackers
12   marshmallows, toasted

1 Place 1 white chocolate half on 1 graham cracker square; top with 2 hot toasted marshmallows and 1 graham cracker square. Repeat with remaining ingredients.

Serves 6.
Preparation time: 10 minutes.
Ready to serve: 10 minutes.
Per serving: 335 calories, 16 g total fat (8.5 g saturated fat), 10 mg cholesterol, 90 mg sodium, 0.5 g fiber.

Menu Tip

• You can also make *Newfangled S'Mores* in the microwave. Heat graham cracker topped with white chocolate and 2 marshmallows in the microwave on High for 20 seconds. Top with remaining graham cracker square.

Before the Event

Assemble the crackers and chocolate on a platter, just waiting for the toasted marshmallows.

LET'S GET COOL AND SPICY

Chill out! This tasty menu won't make you lose your cool. It's easy and fun, and perfect for any warm summer day when a lot of hard work isn't on the agenda, but a great meal is.

Menu

~ Honeydew Prosciutto Bites
~ Mahogany Pork Tenderloin
~ Cool Peanut Noodles
~ Simple Summer Vegetable Stir-Fry
~ White Chocolate Raspberry Tart

Entertains 6

HONEYDEW PROSCIUTTO BITES

Prosciutto is an Italian ham that makes this simple recipe special. If you can't get prosciutto, any smoked ham will still taste terrific with the melon.

1   medium honeydew melon, peeled, seeded
8   oz. prosciutto, sliced paper thin

1 Cut melon into slices, about ½ inch thick; cut each slice in half.

2 Wrap 1 slice of prosciutto around 1 melon piece; secure with toothpick. Repeat with remaining melon and prosciutto.

3 Chill until ready to serve.

Serves 6.
Preparation time: 15 minutes.
Ready to serve: 15 minutes.
Per serving: 160 calories, 6 g total fat (2 g saturated fat), 25 mg cholesterol, 375 mg sodium, 1 g fiber.

Before the Event
Clean and cut the melon the morning of the event.

MAHOGANY PORK TENDERLOIN

Pork tenderloin needs very little time to incorporate the marinade's flavor.

⅓ cup soy sauce
⅓ cup packed brown sugar
1 tablespoon lemon juice
1 teaspoon crushed red pepper
1 lb. pork tenderloin, cut into 1-inch cubes

1 Heat oven to 425°F. Line 15x10x1-inch baking sheet with aluminum foil.

2 In large resealable plastic bag, combine soy sauce, brown sugar, lemon juice and crushed red pepper; seal bag. Toss to combine. Add pork to bag; seal. Toss to combine. Place bag in refrigerator; marinate 15 minutes.

3 Arrange marinated pork on 6 water-soaked bamboo skewers. Place kabobs on baking sheet. Bake 15 minutes or until meat is no longer pink in center and is tender when pierced with a fork.

Serves 6.
Preparation time: 15 minutes.
Ready to serve: 30 minutes.
Per serving: 110 calories, 3 g total fat (1 g saturated fat), 45 mg cholesterol, 260 mg sodium, 0 g fiber.

Menu Tip

• Cut pork cubes the same size so that they cook at the same rate. This is also important for the vegetables in *Simple Summer Vegetable Stir-Fry* (page 178).

Before the Event

Marinate the pork the night before, cover and refrigerate until you're ready to cook.

COOL PEANUT NOODLES

Hoisin, an anise-spiced Asian barbecue sauce, combines with peanut butter to make a delightful sauce for these noodles.

1   (12-oz.) pkg. spaghetti
¼   cup creamy peanut butter
¼   cup hoisin sauce
¼   cup rice vinegar
½   cup hot water
½   cup chopped peanuts

1 Cook spaghetti according to package directions; drain and rinse with cold water. Set aside.

2 Meanwhile, in medium bowl, combine peanut butter, hoisin sauce, rice vinegar and hot water; stir until smooth.

3 In large bowl, toss spaghetti with peanut sauce; top with peanuts.

Serves 6.
Preparation time: 10 minutes.
Ready to serve: 12 minutes.
Per serving: 375 calories, 12.5 g total fat (2 g saturated fat), 0 mg cholesterol, 275 mg sodium, 4.5 g fiber.

Before the Event

Make noodles and sauce a day ahead; refrigerate until you're ready to toss and serve the dish.

SIMPLE SUMMER VEGETABLE STIR-FRY

You barely cook these vegetables to bring out their best flavor and let them retain their

appetizing crispiness.

1   tablespoon vegetable oil
1   red bell pepper, diced
1   carrot, diced
1   yellow squash, diced
2   oz. pea pods, diced
3   green onions, chopped
¼   teaspoon salt
¼   teaspoon freshly ground pepper

1 In wok, heat oil over medium-high heat until hot. Add bell pepper, carrot, squash, pea pods, green onions, salt and pepper; stir-fry about 2 minutes or until vegetables are warmed through but still firm.

Serves 6.
Preparation time: 15 minutes.
Ready to serve: 20 minutes.
Per serving: 40 calories, 2.5 g total fat (0.5 g saturated fat), 0 mg cholesterol, 100 mg sodium, 1.5 g fiber.

Before the Event

Stir-fry vegetables the night before; refrigerate until you're ready to serve.

WHITE CHOCOLATE RASPBERRY TART

Raspberries mean summer, summer means raspberries! This subtle cocoa butter flavor of white chocolate makes a perfect accompaniment to the luscious fruit in this recipe.

1   (8-oz.) pkg. cream cheese, at room temperature
3   oz. white chocolate, melted
1   (9-inch) baked tart shell
2   cups fresh raspberries

1 In medium bowl, combine cream cheese and white chocolate. Spread mixture over tart shell. Top with raspberries.

Serves 6.
Preparation time: 15 minutes.
Ready to serve: 15 minutes.
Per serving: 325 calories, 22.5 g total fat (10 g saturated fat), 60 mg cholesterol, 340 mg sodium, 2.5 g fiber.

Menu Tip

- To make the *White Chocolate Raspberry Tart* even more beautiful, melt about ¼ cup currant jelly in a small pan over low heat. Use a pastry brush to coat the raspberries with warm jelly.

Before the Event

Make *White Chocolate Raspberry Tart* one day ahead, then cover and refrigerate until it's time to serve.

BLOCK PARTY FIESTA

When the whole gang's coming, it's time to do something fun and festive ... a fiesta! Have everyone bring a Mexican condiment such as grated cheese, salsa, sour cream and guacamole to round out this party's simple needs.

Menu

~ Tex Mex Tortellini
~ Zucchini Burritos
~ Summer White Chicken Chili
~ Corn, Pepper and Black Bean Salsa
~ Bizcochitos

Entertains 8

Tex Mex Tortellini

Tortellini is Italian cheese-filled pasta. Taco seasoning transforms it into a Mexican appetizer.

Pasta

1 (9-oz.) pkg. three-cheese tortellini
2 tablespoons dry taco seasoning
1 tablespoon extra-virgin olive oil

Garnish

Sour cream
Salsa
Guacamole

1 In large pot, cook tortellini according to package directions. Drain; rinse with cold water.

2 Place tortellini in large resealable plastic bag; add taco seasoning and oil. Seal; toss to coat.

3 Place tortellini on serving platter. Garnish with sour cream, salsa and guacamole for dipping.

Serves 8.
Preparation time: 5 minutes.
Ready to serve: 10 minutes.
Per serving: 75 calories, 4 g total fat (1 g saturated fat), 25 mg cholesterol, 135 mg sodium, 0.5 g fiber.

Before the Event

Cook tortellini ahead, place in a plastic bag and refrigerate it until ready to use.

ZUCCHINI BURRITOS

These fresh-tasting burritos make good use of summer's most bountiful crop — zucchini.

Filling

1	tablespoon extra-virgin olive oil
½	onion, chopped
4	cups grated zucchini
1	tomato, seeded, chopped
½	cup sliced water chestnuts, drained, rinsed
1	teaspoon ground cumin

Tortilla

16	(8-inch) flour tortillas, warmed

Garnish

2	cups (8 oz.) grated cheddar cheese
	Salsa
	Sour cream
	Guacamole

1 In large skillet, heat oil over medium heat until hot. Add onion; sauté about 2 minutes or until tender.

2 Increase heat to medium-high. Add zucchini, tomato, water chestnuts and cumin to skillet; cook about 2 minutes or until heated through.

3 Serve zucchini mixture in warm flour tortillas topped with grated cheese. Garnish with salsa, sour cream and guacamole.

Serves 8.
Preparation time: 15 minutes.
Ready to serve: 19 minutes.
Per serving: 425 calories, 17.5 g total fat (7 g saturated fat), 30 mg cholesterol, 590 mg sodium, 4 g fiber.

Menu Tip

- *Zucchini Burritos* are best with warmed tortillas. To warm flour tortillas, wrap them in aluminum foil and bake at 325°F for 10 minutes. Or place tortillas on the grill away from direct heat for 10 minutes.

Before the Event

Prepare the burrito filling a day ahead. Drain excess moisture and warm through just before serving.

SUMMER WHITE CHICKEN CHILI

Don't stop making chili just because the weather is warm. You can put together this great summer soup in minutes. It is especially good topped with homemade *Corn, Pepper and Black Bean Salsa* (page 185).

1	tablespoon extra-virgin olive oil
½	onion, chopped
1	(15-oz.) can great northern beans, drained, rinsed
1	(4-oz.) can diced green chiles
2	(14.5-oz.) cans reduced-sodium chicken broth
2	(8- to 12-oz.) cooked chicken breasts, cubed ½ inch thick
1	tablespoon chili powder
1	teaspoon ground cumin
2	cups chopped fresh cilantro

1 In stockpot, heat oil over medium-high heat until hot. Add onion; cook about 2 minutes or until tender.

2 Add beans, chiles, chicken broth, chicken, chili powder, cumin and 1 cup of the cilantro. Reduce heat to medium; cook about 5 minutes or until flavors blend and chili is hot.

3 Serve chili with remaining cilantro. Additional accompaniments could include salsa, sour cream and shredded cheddar cheese.

Serves 8.
Preparation time: 10 minutes.
Ready to serve: 17 minutes.
Per serving: 235 calories, 5 g total fat (1 g saturated fat), 45 mg cholesterol, 560 mg sodium, 6 g fiber.

Before the Event

Make *Summer White Chicken Chili* a day ahead, cover and refrigerate it until ready to warm and serve.

Corn, Pepper and Black Bean Salsa

The beautiful color of this easy salsa makes you want to just eat it *now*! Then you find

out it's as tasty as it is colorful.

1   (15-oz.) can black beans, drained, rinsed
1   (7-oz.) can whole kernel corn, drained
1   red bell pepper, seeded, diced
4   green onions, chopped
2   tablespoons extra-virgin olive oil
    Juice and grated peel of 1 small lime
¼   cup chopped fresh cilantro
⅛   teaspoon salt
⅛   teaspoon freshly ground pepper

1 In medium bowl, combine black beans, corn, bell pepper, green onions, oil, lime juice, lime peel and cilantro; mix well. Season with salt and pepper.

Serves 8.
Preparation time: 15 minutes.
Ready to serve: 15 minutes.
Per serving: 150 calories, 4 g total fat (0.5 g saturated fat), 0 mg cholesterol, 255 mg sodium, 6 g fiber.

Before the Event

Make *Corn, Pepper and Black Bean Salsa* a day ahead, cover and refrigerate until ready to use.

BIZCOCHITOS

Anise-flavored butter cookies end any fiesta with a perfect, sweet note.

1   cup (2 sticks) butter, softened
1   cup sugar
2   tablespoons finely ground anise seeds
2   tablespoons milk
1   teaspoon vanilla extract
2½ cups all-purpose flour

1 Heat oven to 375°F.

2 In large mixing bowl, beat butter and sugar at medium speed about 2 minutes or until fluffy. Mix anise seeds, milk and vanilla until well blended. Gradually beat in flour until well mixed.

3 Roll dough into about 40 (1-inch) balls. Arrange balls on ungreased baking sheet about 2 inches apart; press flat to about ¼ inch thick.

4 Bake 8 minutes or until lightly brown. Cool on baking sheet 1 minute; remove onto wire cooling rack. Repeat with remaining dough.

Serves 8.
Preparation time: 15 minutes.
Ready to serve: 65 minutes.
Per serving: 450 calories, 25 g total fat (14.5 g saturated fat), 60 mg cholesterol, 155 mg sodium, 1.5 g fiber.

Menu Tip
• Press a decorative pattern on top of *Bizcochito* dough with a cookie stamp or imprinted glass.

Before the Event
Prepare the dough for *Bizcochitos* weeks in advance if you wish, and freeze. Bake the day before your fiesta.

INDEX